Facing the Flames

A Fire Fighter's Meditations on the Spiritual Life

BATTALION CHIEF
JOHN STEVENSON, RETIRED

Redeemer Publishing

Hollywood, FL
www.RedeemerPublishing.com

To the men & women of Station 6
Port Everglades
and to those who went before

Other books by John Stevenson:

Doctrines of the Bible: *Outlines in Systematic Theology*
First Corinthians: *Striving for Unity*
Galatians: *Our Freedom in Christ*
Hebrews: *The Supremacy of the Savior*
Luke: *In the Footsteps of the Savior*
Preaching from the Minor Prophets
Romans: *The Radical Righteousness of God*

Table of Contents

Reflection

Since all these things are to be destroyed in this way, what sort of people ought you to be in holy conduct and godliness, looking for and hastening the coming of the day of God, on account of which the heavens will be destroyed by burning, and the elements will melt with intense heat! (2 Peter 3:11-12).

I am a fire fighter. That means a lot of different things to a lot of different people. To my wife, it means concern when she hears about a dangerous situation and knows that I am on duty. She knows what it is like to have gotten a call to tell her that her husband has been injured. To my grandchildren, it means the glamour of riding in a fire truck, although these days I am more likely to be found in a command vehicle. To those under

1

my command, I am the chief, the "old man."

Over the course of my career, I have had the opportunity to save a number of lives and to salvage a number of buildings. It has been a rewarding experience, yet viewed in a different light, there is a certain futility in those endeavors. There is not a person I have saved who will not eventually die. There is not a building I have saved that will not eventually be demolished. My efforts only deal with the temporary and the finite. True significance and security must necessarily encompass more than the mere physical. It is not until we have come to terms with the spiritual life that we have truly faced the flames of life.

Because I am a fire fighter and have been involved in that career for most of my life, I have a tendency to describe and to illustrate spiritual truths in the language of that profession. I have spent a lifetime facing the flame in both senses of the term. These chapters are some of my meditations along the way. My hope is that they will help you as you also face the flames of your own life.

Battalion Chief John Stevenson
2006

Inferno!

But now, thus says the LORD, your Creator, O Jacob, And He who formed you, O Israel, "Do not fear, for I have redeemed you; I have called you by name; you are Mine! When you pass through the waters, I will be with you; and through the rivers, they will not overflow you. When you walk through the fire, you will not be scorched, nor will the flame burn you." (Isaiah 43:1-2).

It was a late afternoon in June and I was just finishing up what had been a rather slow day at the fire station. I was locking the office door and turning to walk out to my car and drive home when my eyes were caught by the black, billowing smoke filling the horizon to the south. Sirens started to sound and all normal people

5

looked and were glad that they were in a position of safety. I am a professional fire fighter and it looked bad enough to know that my short-handed troops would need an extra hand, so I grabbed my fire fighting gear and was on my way.

Smoke was pouring from the roof of a large warehouse and, as I arrived on scene. I gave a hand to a driver engineer who was making some hose connections. I looked up to see a couple of fire fighters putting a ladder to the building and heading to the roof. There were lines being hurriedly laid and I made my way over to where one of my own department's engine crews had a hose line set up along with another line manned by a crew from a neighboring fire department.

"I have to see what is in there," yelled the lieutenant from one of the other departments. Our own captain was there with a two man-crew who were ready to make entry. "John, do you want to take in the team?" I looked at the fiercely billowing smoke that was thrusting its way from the roof of the structure and thought that was the last place that any sane person would go. But they pay me to do this sort of thing, so instead I nodded my head in affirmative and took the nozzle.

My wife asked me once what goes through the mind of a fire fighter on this sort of emergency situation. It isn't something that I had pondered before. Most of our focus is on the job at hand, but there is also a measure of fear that lies somewhere in the back of our minds. It isn't fear of what the fire can do. There isn't usually time for those sorts of reflections. Rather, it is a fear that we might somehow let down the rest of the team.

In this case, I was part of a team of three. Another fire fighter was backing me up and a third was following with a large battle lantern. Normal protocol would have called for an officer to lead us, but in those days our department was underfunded and understaffed. The other hose line was going in and we followed after them. Once inside the door, we found ourselves in a smoke-filled office. Visibility wasn't too bad and we could see a few feet in front of us as we made our way through the twists and turns of the gloomy office. We came to a door that opened into the warehouse and went through it. It was darker in here and one of the fire fighters made his way over to a large garage door. He fiddled with it for a moment and then found the mechanism to open it. A couple of other fire fighters jumped in to help him and soon light was streaming in as the overhead door was raised.

This seemed like a good time to reposition our hose line and we backed it quickly out of the office and then came back in through the open overhead door. Fresh air was sweeping into the warehouse and driving back the smoke so that we could see. It was also a warning sign that we failed to notice as the smoke was sucked back into the depths of the building.

Fire has been likened to a living organism. It grows. It moves. It spreads. And it needs oxygen to breathe. It normally produces smoke and, when a building is on fire, you normally see smoke coming out of the building. On the other hand, when you see the smoke being pulled back into the building, it is a sign that the fire is about to do something bad. The technical term for this is a backdraft. We were about to get a firsthand lesson in this sort of phenomenon.

We advanced both hose lines into the depths of the warehouse and suddenly we stopped, mesmerized by the sight that accosted us. There was a mountain of 55 gallon drums in front of us that seemed to reach all the way to the ceiling that was a very long way above us. Behind them the entire wall seemed to be glowing as giant flames licked over the roof like a spewing volcano. Bang! Bang! Bang! There was a steadily increasing staccato that sounded like machine gun fire -- it was the crashing sound of stressing and exploding drums of flammable acetone.

We opened up our two hose lines, shooting water at that raging inferno, but the fire just seemed to eat up our insignificant water streams. I had never seen so much fire in one place at one time. As I watched, the hose team in front of me closed their line and dropped their hose and nozzle and ran past me. "Let's get out of here!" I heard someone yell. Actually, he added a few colorful and unnecessary words to make his point that much more explicit. Then they were all running past and a wall of smoke and fire was sweeping down on us and enveloping us.

I never thought to drop the nozzle. I had been taught that you hold onto it, no matter what and I did so, even as we turned to follow the other team out of the building.

Suddenly there was a burning heat that cut right through my fire fighting gear as though it did not exist at all. "I'm on fire! I'm burning up!" I heard another fire fighter cry in front of me. I couldn't see him, but I could hear him only a couple of feet from me and I opened up my nozzle in a fog pattern in an effort to cool him down and put out any fire that was actually touching him.

Then I was swept from my feet and the next thing I knew I was lying on the ground outside of the warehouse. Reports from those outside the building said they saw me blown out of the building. I didn't realize this at the time and wasn't certain that I had not tripped over my own feet. The nozzle was still in my hands, but my helmet had been ripped off, its strap literally torn from the supporting rivet and my air mask was pulled sideways on my face, spilling air from the openings. I tried to shut the flow of leaking water from the nozzle, but my left arm would not work. I reached the nozzle with my right hand and closed it the rest of the way down and then straightened my mask on my face. There was still thick, black smoke streaming past me from the explosion.

Then other fire fighters were beside me, helping me to my feet and out of the way of the open doorway. There was a sharp pain in my ribs.

I tried to pull my air pack off, but my left arm was still hanging uselessly and I needed help to get the pack and my fire fighting coat off. Then I was being hustled over to some paramedics who hustled me into a medical unit and rushed me off to the local hospital. I hadn't been at the hospital more than 15 or 20 minutes when I was joined by two other fire fighters suffering from a bit of smoke inhalation. I was lucky. I had been spared this by wearing breathing gear the entire time I had been inside. X-rays were taken and I found that I had somehow broken one of the bones in my shoulder blade. The doctor said it was a bit unusual and the injury could only be accounted by having something hit me from behind.

This was the biggest and most spectacular fire that South Florida had seen in many a year. News footage was shown across the country and I received calls from all over. Years later I would continue to see footage from the fire aired at training seminars throughout the world.

The G.L.S. fire has been used as an excellent example of what not to do. There were no safety officers, no real plan that was communicated to all of those present and no one who was in charge of all of the operations. There were as many as six different fire departments involved in battling the blaze and, to be fair, they did manage to save the majority of the building. It still stands there as I write this account many years later. But the outcome could easily have been very different. Mine was the worst injury --

I was out of work for a month or two as I waited for the bones to heal in my shoulder and back. Years later it would still ache a bit when the weather turned cold.

You can go through life with no real plan and without recognizing that the God of the universe is in charge and it may look like things are going well. But when the flames of failure race across your world and things go to hell in a hand basket, then you come to the glaring conclusion that your life is serving as a living image of what not to do.

This book is written to tell you that there is a better way. Because I've served over 25 years as a professional fire fighter, I'll be phrasing a lot of what I have to say in terms of the career where I've spent so much of my life. But the same truths apply to you, no matter what your chosen profession.

Bad things happen in this life. We didn't need to see the Twin Towers of the World Trade Center fall down to teach us this basic lesson. Just look at the regular business of any funeral parlor and you will see the same truth. Life can be hard and then you die. Even if you manage to get through most of the trials of this life relatively unscathed, death still is waiting at the end.

As I said, there is a better way. It is found in the Bible. God gave us a preplan for life and for death and, if we learn its lessons now, we will be ready for those lessons in the future. This book is designed to teach us some of those lessons.

If you are a fire fighter, then I am sure that you have plenty of your own "war stories" that would just as effectively illustrate these sorts of spiritual life lessons. Perhaps this book can help you to gain a new perspective on those experiences. And if you are not a fire fighter, then I invite you to join me for what has been an exciting and fulfilling adventure -- the spiritual life that is found in Jesus Christ.

Rescue Me!

Stretch forth Thy hand from on high;
Rescue me and deliver me out of great
waters (Psalm 144:7a).

Chauncey Naylor was something of a trouble-shooter. As a Lieutenant under my command, he could be relied upon to think on his feet and come up with innovative ideas in difficult situations. But there comes a time when all of the innovation and personal resources in the world are just not enough. Chauncey met with such a situation in the middle of the Atlantic Ocean.

He had taken a special assignment with a salvage crew that was responding to a large freighter that had broken up in heavy seas. Instead of sinking, a large section of the hull was still afloat and was therefore a hazard to navigation. The job of the salvage crew was to go aboard and find a way to sink the derelict. They never made it.

15

The crew had flown down to the Dominican Republic and then had boarded an ocean-going tug that was hired to take the team out to the derelict. Tired from his long flight, Chauncey was catching up on some much-needed sleep when a crew member rushed into his cabin, grabbed a life jacket and then rushed back out without saying a word. Curious as to these actions, Chauncey pulled on some clothes and went out to investigate. What he saw was cause for concern. The tugboat was taking on water in the heavy seas and it would only be a matter of minutes before it sank beneath the crashing waves. A call for help was quickly transmitted and the crew were looking for any extra life jackets or floatation devices.

All too soon, the deck tilted up at a perilous angle and Chauncey and the rest of the crew took to the water so as not to be pulled beneath the waves. They had a single rubber raft that was far too small to accommodate all of them and which was quickly filled with water from the huge crashing waves. They held to the sides of the raft so as not to drift apart and be lost from one another. They were quickly seasick from the continually trashing motion of the breakers. Weak and dazed, there was nothing to do but to hold on and to hope for eventual rescue.

A Mayday call had gone out for rescue but, unbeknown to them, the strong current was pulling them quickly from the location where their vessel had first sent out its distress call. An hour passed and then two and three. In the distance, they could make out search and rescue helicopters sweeping over the storm-tossed sea, but none came close.

It had been midmorning when the sinking had first taken place and they hung on grimly throughout the day, sick and weak and barely hanging on for life. Afternoon came and went and the light of day was starting to fade and, with it, any hopes of rescue. Some of the men were in worse shape than others and Chauncey realized that not all of the crew would survive the night. In the last couple hours of fading light, a United States Coast Guard helicopter came their way. They had latched onto a palm branch and they took this and used it to wave a small piece of plastic in hopes of attracting the pilot's attention. They later learned that the pilot of the helicopter had not yet begun his search and was still en route to the search grid. He happened to spot the movement out of the corner of his eye. They watched from below as the helicopter swept past them and then suddenly veered around to come and hover over them. Within a few minutes, a rescue basket was being lowered to them and they were plucked up out of the water. They were saved. They were lifted from the place of danger and they were transported to the place of safety.

Imagine for a moment if there had been a different ending to the story. Imagine that the rescuers in the helicopter came and hovered over those in need of rescue and called down to them, "You are doing quite well. Just keep swimming in a westerly direction for about 600 miles and you should reach Miami." We would not think very highly of such a rescue effort. We would not classify such assistance as a rescue. We might call such a person an encourager, but he can hardly be described as a rescuer.

Or imagine that one of the rescuers in the helicopter dives into the water and demonstrates the breaststroke. He shows how to keep one's head above water and he even gives to each one of those in the water a manual entitled, "How to swim in ten easy lessons." Such a person might be seen as teacher and even as an example, but he is not a rescuer.

Or imagine that the rescuers take the waterlogged crew into their helicopter and then fly them to a point within 20 miles of land before throwing them out again. "You are now a lot closer than you were before," points out the helicopter crew. They may have been a help and an assistance, but they still fall short of being a rescuer.

A rescuer is much more than an encourager or a teacher or an assistant in time of need. A rescuer is one who takes you all the way to shore. He takes you from your place of need and he brings you to a place of safety.

The Bible teaches us that we are in need of a rescuer. We are adrift in this world and we are unable to rescue ourselves. Left alone, we will all one day die and face the judgment of God.

It is appointed for men to die once
and after this comes judgment

18

(Hebrews 9:27).

The good news of the Bible is that there is a Rescuer. Not merely an encourager or a good teacher or even an assistant, but One who has brought about a cosmic rescue operation. His name is Jesus and He gave His life for us upon the cross.

The Bible teaches us that Jesus was born and grew to manhood and then, as an adult, died upon the cross in order to be a sacrifice for our sins. He died that we might live. His death brings about my rescue.

How can I be rescued? What is required on my part to affirm my rescue? Nothing. Merely to place my faith and confidence -- myself -- into the hands of my Rescuer, entrusting myself to Him.

There is an old story that tells of a man who was traveling on his donkey when he came upon a small fuzzy object lying in the road. He dismounted to look more closely and found a sparrow lying on its back with its scrawny legs thrust upward. At first he thought the bird was dead, but closer investigation proved it to be very much alive. The man asked the sparrow if he was all right. The sparrow replied, "Yes." The man asked, "What are you doing lying on your back with your legs pointed towards the sky?" The sparrow responded that he had heard a rumor that the sky was falling, and so he was holding his legs up to catch it. The man retorted, "You surely don't think that you're going to hold it up with those two scrawny legs, do you?" The sparrow, with a very solemn look, replied, "One does the best he can."

Our problem is like the problem of the sparrow. We might try to do the best we can, but our best is not good enough. Indeed, our most noble efforts seem altogether puny compared with what is really needed. When the sky is falling, our reaction might be to lift our hands to stop it, but it will do us no good.

The issue here is not the falling of the sky, but the falling of God's judgment. Man's natural response is not to lift his arms or his legs, but his good deeds in an effort to save himself. The Bible teaches that salvation is an act of God's free grace.

> *For by grace you have been saved through faith; and that not of yourselves, it is the gift of God; not as a result of works, so that no one may boast. (Ephesians 2:8-9).*

This passage contrasts both how we have been saved and how we have not been saved. We are not saved through our own efforts or as a result of our own works. We are not saved by anything in ourselves that is worthy of boasting. One who is rescued cannot boast about how good a victim he was. He can only boast about the wonderful deed of the Rescuer.

We are saved "by grace." That means we

are saved without having contributed to the reason for our salvation. While this is related to mercy, I believe it to be more than mercy. Mercy is when you are pulled over by a policeman for doing 50 miles per hour in a zone where the speed limit is 30 - and he does not give you a ticket. By contrast, grace is when that same policeman not only refrains from giving you a ticket but also invites you over to his house for dinner. You have been saved by grace. You do not deserve to be saved. You cannot earn this salvation. It is a free gift.

How about you? Have you been rescued? Or are you merely hanging onto whatever happens to float by? There is a Rescuer who calls you to turn to Him and call out to be rescued. This is a matter of faith.

There are three elements in faith. The first element of faith is knowledge. Faith must have some root in fact or else it is mere wistful thinking. There must be some objective fact which is to be believed. Our faith is not in faith. There is an object to our faith. The object of our faith is Jesus Christ. We believe that He died for us and that He was buried and that He rose again. And we believe that His death and burial and resurrection had a result of purchasing our salvation.

The second element of faith is appropriation. Knowing that Christ died is a mere knowledge of a historical event. Salvation requires knowing that He died for me. I must appropriate that sacrifice that He made and see

21

that it was on my own behalf.

The third element of faith is commitment. This is where I accept Him as my Lord and Savior. It involves casting myself upon Christ, resting on His promises, and joining His forever family.

When Chauncey Naylor and his crew were spotted in the stormy waters of the Atlantic, the rescue helicopter dropped a basket down to them. At that point, they had a decision to make. It was not an overly difficult decision. They could remain where they were in the churning waters, or they could entrust themselves into the hands of their rescuers.

It would not have been enough for Chauncey to call up to the helicopter and to say, "I believe your helicopter is aerodynamically constructed so that it can carry people to safety." He had to commit himself to the safety basket. He had to get into the helicopter. He had to appropriate the salvation that had come his way.

Faith in Jesus means that we join ourselves to Him. We commit ourselves to Him as our only hope for salvation. We give ourselves into His keeping and He promises to do the rest. Have you done that? Have you entrusted yourself to Him?

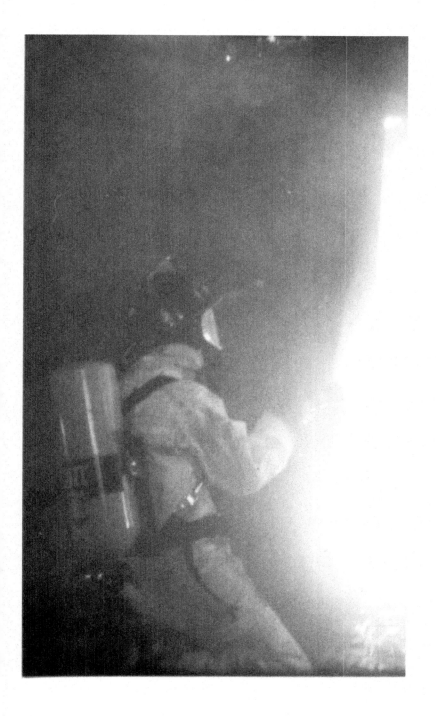

Finding God in the Darkness

Then they cried out to the LORD
in their trouble;
He saved them out of their distresses.
He brought them out of darkness and the
shadow of death,
And broke their bands apart. (Psalm
107:13-14).

The morning sky had not yet begun to pale in the east when the crew aboard the cargo ship noticed that there was something dreadfully wrong aboard their vessel. Plumes of thick, acrid smoke were already pouring from one of the passageways, driving the crew out onto the main deck. Luckily, the vessel was moored at the dock and a crew member was dispatched to the shore to notify the fire department. He found a pay phone but then stopped, for he was unaware of the simple 911 system that is common to the United States. He simply did not know what number to call. What he did know was that the fire station was located on the main road into the seaport, nearly two miles from where his ship was docked. He had no car or other means of transportation, so he ran the entire distance.

Because of the delay, the fire had been given plenty of time to intensify and to heat up by the time we arrived on the scene. Luckily, it was located amidships on the main deck and so had been unable to move into the cargo holds or down into the engine room. Nevertheless, it was a hot fire as our crews dragged their hoselines up the gangway, across the deck and into the superstructure of the vessel. The fire had long since flashed over the cabin where the fire originated and was now rolling across the passageways; not that we could see much in the way of flames. The smoke was thick and black and came all the way down to the floor.

The lead hose team only made it partway to the fire when they ran short of air and called for a relief team to follow the hose to the nozzle and take over. I was on the relief team and checked in with the nozzleman, relieving him on the nozzle amidst the clattering of alarm bells from low air packs. Our instructions were to standby until a backup hose team caught up to us and so, we held place in the thick, black smoke, using an occasional short burst of water to darken down the flames that were rolling over our heads.

I felt a gloved hand on my shoulder and heard the words, "I'll be right back," from my partner on the hoseline and suddenly I was alone in the darkness. This wasn't the way things were supposed to happen. Freelancing is forbidden in the fire service and even back in those early days of my career it was not approved. I was a bit torn between obeying my orders to remain in place versus doing the safe thing and pulling out. I decided to remain.

Every fire fighter who has been on the job for any length of time has found himself in a situation where he is down on his hands and knees in a place where he cannot see his hand in front of his face. I knew this was the case because I had checked with a gloved hand. It is at a time like this that a sense of introspection arises and one is faced with the existential question: "What on earth am I doing here?"

You may be asking yourself the same question. True, the darkness that you are facing in your life is probably not literal, but you can nevertheless empathize with that lonely feeling of abandonment and you long for the hand of God upon your shoulder that whispers, "It's okay, I am with you."

Those were the words that Moses heard. He had been alone for a very long time. Wanted for the murder of an Egyptian taskmaster, he had long since left the land of his birth to become a fugitive in the wilderness. He had gone from a prince of Egypt to a lowly shepherd. He had gone from the glories of the land of the pyramids to what felt like the wasted life of a desert nomad. There must have been times when he asked the question, "What on earth am I doing here?"

One day, Moses happened upon an unusual sight. It was a fire. At the source of the fire was a bush. He must have watched for a while, waiting for the bush to be consumed by the fire. Perhaps an hour passed and then another. The fire showed no signs of dying down. The bush showed no signs of burning. The leaves were still green and visible through the flames.

Suddenly there was a voice.

"Moses, Moses!"

What do you say to a talking bush? I can't think of a better reply than the one Moses gives, "Here I am!" What follows is a conversation, not between a bush and a man, but between the God of all the universe and His chosen servant.

To be sure, Moses isn't sure that he is up

to the task, especially when he learns that it involves going back to Egypt. Egypt? That is the one place on earth where he doesn't want to go. It is the place of scandal. It is the place where he has been accused of a heinous crime. Moses knows deep down in his heart that the accusation is true. It is bad enough to have people accuse you; it is even worse when you know the accusation is on target.

God sets forth the plan. Moses is to go to Egypt and he will be the spokesman for God. The Lord will give the message and Moses will proclaim it.

Moses must have wondered why he was necessary to the plan. After all, God could simply have spoken to Pharaoh and the people of Egypt from a burning bush or from a storm cloud or from a pillar of fire. Why did Moses have to get involved? It is because God wanted to get personal.

The story is told of a little girl who cried out to her mother from her bedroom, "Mommy, I'm afraid to be in my dark room alone." Her mother replied, "It's okay, Honey. The Lord is with you." She called back, "Yes, but I want someone with skin on."

Throughout the Old Testament, God had manifested Himself in thunder and lightning, a cloud by day and a pillar of fire by night. He had approached men through a sacrificial system, by the blood of bulls and of goats. There was a mediator in the priesthood and a holy place in the Temple - and before that, the Tabernacle. But ultimately there was something lacking in all of these manifestations. There was a desire to experience God "with skin on." Jesus is God "with skin on." He has come so that we never have to be afraid again.

That means when we come to the Lord, we come to One who understands. We come to One who has experienced all the doubts, the fears, and even the temptations we regularly face. He is the One who comes to us in the midst of our own darkness and who tells us that we are not alone.

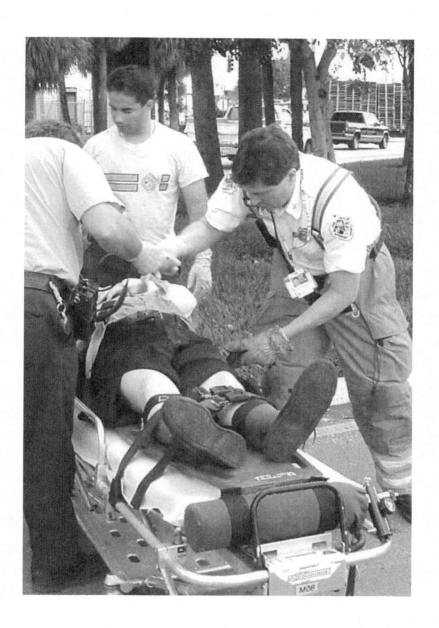

Facing the Flame of God

Our God is a consuming fire (Hebrews 12:29).

If you have ever sat before a late night campfire, you know that there is something almost hypnotic about watching the flickering of a flame. It seems to move with a life of its own, first flickering this way and then its tongues of fire reaching out that way. It moves and it breathes and it ebbs and flows like a living thing.

There are a number of occasions in which the Bible describes God in terms of a fire. We have already seen the image of the burning bush that confronted Moses in the wilderness. The thing that made that sight so remarkable was not that the bush was burning, but that it was not consumed by the fire.

Yet we must not forget that God's flame often does consume that which it touches. Again and again, the Scriptures remind us that God is a consuming fire.

> *So watch yourselves, lest you forget the covenant of the LORD your God, which He made with you, and make for yourselves a graven image in the form of anything against which the LORD your God has commanded you. For the LORD your God is a consuming fire, a jealous God. (Deuteronomy 4:23-24).*

The point is made that we ought to take care against forgetting our promises to God and against taking God too lightly because He is a consuming fire.

The Bible could have said that God is a warming fire. It could have looked at the emotional comfort that we can feel when we think of God's protection and His love for His people. We come into His presence for the warmth that He provides.

Or the Bible could have said that God is an enlightening fire. His presence provides light so that those who dwell in darkness are able to see reality in a clear and vivid way. He is the light of the world and we can see things more clearly when we are in His presence.

The Bible also could have described God

as a purifying fire. When we come to Him, he burns away all of the trivia from our lives and He purifies us by removing that which hinders our relationship to Him.

God is all of these things. He is warming and He is enlightening and He is purifying. But there is another quality of God that is presented in the Bible. It is that He is a consuming fire. He comes and He consumes that with which He is displeased.

In my career as a fire fighter, I've had the opportunity to see what a fire can do. I've seen fires consume vehicles and buildings and people until nothing is left but charred ash. These experiences have provided a vivid lesson as to the consuming power of fire. In a similar way, the Old Testament prophet Isaiah received a vivid image of the consuming power of God. He tells us of a glorious vision of God's glory.

> *In the year of King Uzziah's death, I saw the Lord sitting on a throne, lofty and exalted, with the train of His robe filling the temple. Seraphim stood above Him, each having six wings; with two he covered his face, and with two he covered his feet, and with two he flew. And one called out to another and said, "Holy, Holy, Holy, is the LORD of hosts, The whole earth is full of His glory." And the foundations of the*

thresholds trembled at the voice of him who called out, while the temple was filling with smoke. (Isaiah 6:1-4).

Isaiah's vision is of the Lord in his temple. He is attended by Seraphim. That isn't a word we use today outside of Christmas carols. It comes to us from the Hebrew word *saraph* which means "to burn." God is described as being flanked by these "burning ones." That they are described in such a manner should not surprise us, for the Bible elsewhere speaks of how God's angels are "a flame of fire" (Hebrews 1:7).

The idea of winged supernatural beings was not unknown in the ancient world. Statues of four-footed winged beasts can be found throughout ancient Mesopotamia and Persia. Note that the passage does not say that they were human in appearance, but only that they had six wings and the power of speech.

Isaiah calls our attention to the announcement which the heavenly messengers proclaim before the throne of God. First comes the threefold announcement of the holiness of God. And then comes the statement that...

"The whole earth is full of His glory" (Isaiah 6:3).

What does this mean? In what way is the whole earth full of the glory of God? It should be noted that this is not the first time that such a statement had been made. The Lord said this of Himself to Moses in the Wilderness after the Israelites had sinned by listening to the pessimistic report of the ten spies.

> *So the Lord said, "I have pardoned them according to your word; but indeed, as I live, ALL THE EARTH SHALL BE FILLED WITH THE GLORY OF THE LORD." (Numbers 14:20-21).*

Up to that time, Moses had seen the presence of the Lord in the burning bush and the Israelites had seen the glory of the Lord and His power manifested in the Exodus Event. But the Lord is not going to limit His dealings to Israel. His glory will be seen by all the earth. The phrase is repeated in the form of a prayer in one of David's Psalms.

> *Blessed be the Lord God, the God of Israel,*
> *Who alone works wonders.*
> *And blessed be His glorious name forever;*
> *And may the WHOLE EARTH BE FILLED WITH HIS GLORY.*
> *Amen, and Amen. (Psalm 72:18-19).*

This Psalm calls for all the nations to worship the Lord (Psalm 72:17). As that universal worship takes place, so also will take place the filling of the earth with the glory of God. On the other hand, Isaiah's vision does not describe this in terms of a future prophecy. The angelic announcement speaks of it as a present reality. It is spoken of as though it had already come to pass.

Perhaps that is because the process had already begun. I believe that the process still continues today. The earth today is being filled with the glory of God. Every time another person comes to Christ and becomes a worshiper of God, there is that much more of God's glory filling the earth. Isaiah sees himself coming into that process of becoming a worshiper of God in a most dramatic way.

> *Then I said, "Woe is me, for I am ruined! Because I am a man of unclean lips, And I live among a people of unclean lips; For my eyes have seen the King, the LORD of hosts." (Isaiah 6:5).*

Isaiah was not unmoved by the heavenly vision. His first reaction was an increased sense of his own sinfulness. That is what happens when you have an encounter with the flame of God. A proper God-concept will always lead to a proper self-concept. If you look at yourself and cannot see your sin, it is because you haven't really seen the Lord.

I am not saying that we should go around

looking at our sin all the time or that this should be our main focus in life. I am saying that a right view of God will eliminate personal pride or a sense that we can approach Him on the basis of our own merits.

There is an interesting flow of reaction seen in this chapter. One moment, Isaiah is saying, "Woe is me, I am a ruined sinner with unclean lips." By the time we get to verse 8, he shall be saying, "Here am I, send me to speak on your behalf!" What made the difference? It is seen in the forgiveness of verses 6-7.

> *Then one of the seraphim flew to me, with a burning coal in his hand which he had taken from the altar with tongs. And he touched my mouth with it and said, "Behold, this has touched your lips; and your iniquity is taken away, and your sin is forgiven." (Isaiah 6:6-7).*

This is a wonderful scene. Isaiah has just become aware of his own sinfulness. He confesses that he has unclean lips. But then a cleaning of his lips takes place. The source is that of a burning coal from the altar.

Do you see it? The cleansing power to stand in the presence of God comes from God Himself. He is righteous and He demands righteousness, but He is also the solution to His own demand.

The picture of the altar is ultimately fulfilled in the person of Jesus. He is the One who offered Himself as a sacrifice for sins. It is through faith in Him that we are made right with God. It is by our faith encounter with Him that our iniquity is taken away and our sins are forgiven.

> *Then I heard the voice of the Lord, saying, "Whom shall I send, and who will go for Us?" Then I said, "Here am I. Send me!" (Isaiah 6:8).*

The message of forgiveness demands a response on the part of the forgiven. Thus when the call goes out for one to be a representative of the Lord, Isaiah is quick to volunteer. He finds himself chosen and commissioned by God.

> *And He said,*
> *"Go, and tell this people:*
> *Keep on listening, but do not perceive;*
> *Keep on looking, but do not understand.*
> *Render the hearts of this people insensitive, their ears dull, and their eyes dim,*
> *Lest they see with their eyes, hear with their ears, understand with their hearts, and return and be healed."*
> *Then I said, "Lord, how long?"*
> *And He answered,*
> *"Until cities are devastated and without*

inhabitant,
houses are without people and the land is
utterly desolate,
the Lord has removed men far away, and
the forsaken places are many in the midst
of the land.
Yet there will be a tenth portion in it,
and it will again be subject to burning,
like a terebinth or an oak whose stump
remains when it is felled.
The holy seed is its stump." (Isaiah 6:9-
13).

Isaiah is given a commission from the Lord. It is not a commission to be successful or to build a large congregation or to develop a large following. Indeed, the Lord tells Isaiah that he will do none of these things. His preaching will have just the opposite effect. It will...

(1) Render their **hearts** insensitive.
   (2) Render their **ears** dull.
      (3) Render their **eyes** dim.
      (3) Lest they see with their **eyes**.
   (2) Lest they hear with their **ears**.
(1) Lest they understand with their **hearts**,

This poetic circle is presented to show the futility of those who hear the truth but who are not changed by it. This is the bad news. It is that Isaiah's preaching will leave most people unaffected. The effect that it will have upon many will be only to harden them further from the truth. But there is also good news. It is that there will be a remnant. This remnant is described in the terms of a *tithe*, a tenth portion.

Earlier in the book of Isaiah, he described Israel as the vineyard of the Lord. In those chapters, the Lord spoke of the BRANCH of the Lord that would be beautiful and glorious (Isaiah 4:1). Now we see the ancient nation of God described as a stump. There is a difference between a branch and a stump. A branch is something living. It is alive because it is connected to the tree. But a stump exists because death has taken place. Something necessary has been cut off. The point of the prophecy is that the nation would be cut down in judgment. That is the bad news. But the good news is that God can produce living seed even from a burnt-out stump.

He did, you know. The nation of Israel was destroyed. The Northern Kingdom of Israel was taken into captivity in Isaiah's day. The Southern Kingdom of Judah lasted 150 years longer. But it was also eventually destroyed. From that destruction, God preserved His holy seed. A new Israel grew up from it - an Israel that eventually gave birth to Jesus Christ - the Messiah. This is the ultimate fulfillment of Isaiah's prophecy. Indeed, the words of this very chapter are referenced in the Gospel of John:

> *But though He had performed so many signs before them, yet they were not believing in Him; that the word of Isaiah the*

42

prophet might be fulfilled, which he spoke, "LORD, who has believed our report? And to whom has the arm of the Lord been revealed?"

For this cause they could not believe, for Isaiah said again, "He has blinded their eyes, and He hardened their heart; lest they see with their eyes, and perceive with their heart, and be converted, and I heal them."

These things Isaiah said, because he saw His glory, and he spoke of Him. (John 12:37-41).

Do you see it? The prophecy of Isaiah was speaking ultimately of JESUS. He is the One whom Isaiah saw when he *saw His glory, and he spoke of Him.* He is the One of whom all of the Old Testament prophets described. He is the One who came with the strength of the arm of the Lord. That arm was flexed to the max when Jesus went to the cross and died in our place and then rose again to show that death had been defeated.

Have you come to the flame of God? Have you found the warmth, the light, the purification and even the consuming power that it provides? You can do so by coming to Jesus, for He is the flame of God personified. He is the one of whom it was said, *We beheld His glory, glory as of the only begotten from the Father, full of grace and truth (John 1:14).*

Facing the Flame
of Temptation

Take up the shield of faith
with which you will be able to
extinguish all the flaming missiles
of the evil one (Ephesians 6:16).

It was four in the morning when the alarm
came in. It was a rollover involving a gasoline
tank truck. Even though we had trained for this
sort of call on countless occasions and even
though we had responded to similar emergency
situations, there was still a charge of adrenalin as
we responded to the scene.

As we first arrived, I surveyed the scene
and gave a quick size-up. A gasoline tank truck
had been maneuvering alongside the side of some
railroad tracks and had gotten too close to the

nearby drainage ditch. Both the tank and the tractor hauling it had rolled over into the ditch that was more of a shallow canal at this time of year.

As I established command and called for more units to respond, one of my engine companies did a quick reconnaissance of the area. The other team laid out protective hose lines from the scene back to a fire hydrant that was sufficiently distant from the site of the accident to provide a measure of safety. We had plenty of fire fighting foam in both of our industrial fire pumpers, but it would be better if the volatile fuel did not find an ignition source.

The recon team reported that the hatch covers were all in place and that there was very little leakage taking place. A bit of explanation is in order. Gasoline tank trucks are equipped with hatches on the top of the tank. When a tank has rolled over onto its side, those covers are now on the side of the tank and subject to leakage. Though they have seals, it does not take much for one to fail and to spill out the contents of the tank.

The only way to remedy the situation is to secure the lids and then to drill a series of holes into what is now the highest portion of the tank so that a suction tube can be inserted and the hazardous flammable liquid transferred out. My crews were familiar with the operation and had practiced it on any number of occasions.

Once the protective foam lines were in place, I sent in a crew to secure the hatch covers with special clamps designed for that purpose.

The crew reported a problem. They could not reach one of the dome covers because it was hanging over the canal into which the tank had fallen.

Fire crew drills a petroleum tank during a training drill.

I had a decision to make. I could either wait until a boat could be obtained and hope that my fire fighters could then use that as a platform on which to stand as they secured the last hatch, or else I could proceed with the off loading operation and hope that the seals held without any additional clamps. Since it had been reported to me that there was currently a bare minimum of leakage, I chose the latter option.

By this time, I had assembled a large collection of fire engines from the surrounding fire departments, all of whom were eager to assist as a part of our mutual aid system. I appointed units to various groups and divisions so that my span of control would not be too great. By this time, the sun had come up.

As the sun rose higher and higher into the sky, we were faced first with one delay and then another. The chief whom I had appointed as safety officer expressed some concerns over the stability of the tank. Would it begin to roll once it was off loaded? The Technical Rescue Team was on scene and worked at stabilizing the tank. Once this one done, my entry team moved up to begin drilling the tank. Now a disturbing report came in. The leak which before had been only a small drip was now growing into a steady trickle. What was causing it? The answer was obvious. The heat of the sun on the shell of the tank was causing the gasoline inside to expand. The added pressure was pushing against the seals of the tank lids and threatening to compromise them.

The danger that we faced during that scene illustrates a corresponding danger that people face when a temptation is permitted to go unchallenged and unchecked. This is vividly seen in the case of the very first temptation in history.

You are probably familiar with the story.

God created the first man and put him into a luscious garden with plenty of food and water and a companion fitted for him. There was only one condition.

> *And the Lord God commanded the man, saying, "from any tree of the garden you may eat freely; but from the tree of the knowledge of good and evil you shall not eat, for in the day that you eat from it you shall surely die." (Genesis 2:16-17).*

This condition gave man the freedom to choose for God or against God. He could obey and live or he could disobey and die. Genesis 3 tells the story of what man did with that freedom.

> *Now the serpent was more crafty than any beast of the field which the Lord God had made. And he said to the woman, "Indeed, has God said, 'You shall not eat from any tree of the garden'?"*
>
> *And the woman said to the serpent, "From the fruit of the trees of the garden we may eat; 3 but from the fruit of the tree which is in the midst of the garden, God has said, 'You shall not eat from it or touch it, lest you die.'"*

And the serpent said to the woman, "You surely shall not die! 5 For God knows that in the day you eat from it your eyes will be opened, and you will be like God, knowing good and evil."

When the woman saw that the tree was good for food, and that it was a delight to the eyes, and that the tree was desirable to make one wise, she took from its fruit and ate, and she gave also to her husband with her, and he ate. (Genesis 3:1-6).

There are several things which we ought to note from this passage. First of all, notice that the temptation came from an outside source. There was nothing within them to tempt themselves. Allow me to let you in on a secret. I don't need an outside source to tempt me to sin. And neither do you. I have something within me that likes sin — that finds sin fun. It isn't that the "devil made me do it." It is that I wanted to do it.

We call this a sin nature. It is an orientation to sin. But Adam and Eve were not created in this way. They had no orientation to sin. They had the ability to choose not to sin. And so, their choice to sin was all the more despicable.

Secondly, note that the temptation began at different levels. Instead of immediately contradicting the word of God, the serpent began by questioning the word of God: Did God really say that? The temptation focused upon the limitation of God's command rather than the graciousness of God's provision. The serpent did not point out that Adam and Eve were free to eat of every tree of the garden. Rather it was the restriction that became the object of the temptation.

The lie of Satan was to assign ungracious and unloving motives to God. This always takes place when you are tempted. All temptation involves the idea that you can obtain something for yourself that God is denying you.

By the way, a surface reading of the passage seems to indicate that the Serpent told the truth. Their eyes were opened. They did come to and experiential understanding of good and evil. And most importantly, they didn't die, at least not in the physical sense and not immediately, although the process of death indeed began that day. Temptation often involves focusing on a portion of the truth. Even a stopped clock is right twice a day and the devil's counterfeits often contain a portion of truth. It only takes a spoonful of arsenic added to an entire glass of water to render the entire potion poisonous.

These series of temptations went unchallenged and unchecked by the woman. What is more, it seems possible that they also went unchallenged and unchecked by the man. This is seen when we take another look at the latter part of verse 6 - *she gave also to her husband **with her**, and he ate*. Was the man with her during the entire series of temptations? I do not know. But there is no mention of his challenging these temptations or resisting them.

> *No temptation has overtaken you but such as is common to man; and God is faithful, who will not allow you to be tempted beyond what you are able, but with the temptation will provide the way of escape also, that you may be able to endure it. (1 Corinthians 10:13).*

We have a strong word of encouragement. It is that God has made provision for us in our hour of temptation. God will never take you into a tunnel that does not have a light at the end of it. He will never take you into the valley of the shadow of death without being with you.

This passage tells us there is a commonality of temptation: *No temptation has overtaken you but such as is common to man (10:13).* You won't necessarily believe this when you are in the midst of temptation, so I want you to learn this principle now. It is that your temptations are not unique. Whatever you are going through has been experienced by millions of other people just like you. You are not alone. Even Jesus experienced those same temptations.

> *For we do not have a high priest who cannot sympathize with*

our weaknesses, but One who has been tempted in all things as we are, yet without sin. (Hebrews 4:15).

Jesus was tempted *in all things as we are.* Everything that you go through, He went through. He understands your problems because He experienced them. This means He is qualified to help you.

This passage also reminds us of the faithfulness of God in temptation: *God is faithful, who will not allow you to be tempted beyond what you are able (10:13).* The reason you do not need to fear temptation is because God is faithful. Even when you are faithless, God is still faithful. He designed you. He knows you better than you know yourself. He knows your stress limit. He knows exactly how much you can take and He has promised not to exceed that limit.

This means you have no excuse to sin. You can't say, "The devil made me do it." Satan cannot make you sin. If you sin, then it is because you decided to sin. Don't ever try to blame God because of your sin. He has made a way of escape.

This passage promises a way of escape from temptation: *God is faithful, who will not allow you to be tempted beyond what you are able, but with the temptation will provide the way of escape also, that you may be able to endure it (10:13).*

I have spent many years as a fire fighter.

It was my job to put out fires. One of the things that I learned was never to go into a burning building unless there is a way out of that building. More often than not, we look for several different means of exiting a building in case one is cut off.

God makes the same provision for me. In the heat of the battle and when the smoke is all around us, He says, "Don't worry, I've put you here and I've got your escape route open." How can we escape temptation? There are several steps.

- Resolve to resist temptation. We are promised in James 4:7, *resist the devil and he will flee from you.* Remember the story of Joseph as a slave in Potiphar's house. Potiphar's wife developed a physical infatuation for him and sought his affection. When he refused her advances, she persisted and went so far as to grab hold of him. Joseph had resolved not to allow himself to be tempted.

  The sin that Joseph faced is a common one in today's society. We live in a land where immoral living is the norm and where such sins have become socially acceptable. We are warned in the Scriptures against this sort of behavior.

  Can a man take fire in his bosom,
  And his clothes not be burned?
  Or can a man walk on hot coals,
  And his feet not be scorched?

So is the one who goes in to his
neighbor's wife;
Whoever touches her will not go
unpunished. (Proverbs 6:27-29).

The New Testament uses this same
fiery language in 1 Corinthians 7:9 to
describe the temptations of those who are
tempted with premarital relationships.

• Use the Scriptures. That is what Jesus did
  when He was tempted by the devil in the
  wilderness. We read of three different
  temptations and in all three cases, Jesus
  responded by quoting the Scriptures back
  to the devil.

  Thy word I have treasured in my
  heart,
  That I may not sin against Thee.
  (Psalm 119:11).

• Use your position. Paul says that we are
  to consider ourselves dead to sin. We
  have been crucified with Christ and we
  are to have an outlook that reckons our
  past life of sinfulness to have been dead
  and buried. Returning to a life of sin is
  like a resurrected person returning to the
  coffin from which he was raised. We are
  not to live there any longer.

• Use the cross. When you are tempted,

remember that Jesus died for the very sort of sins to which you are being tempted. Go back to the shadow of the cross and look at the One who died in your place. Remember that His death calls for a response on how you are to live today.

- Devote your thoughts to think God's thoughts. Remember that sin is not only that which is outward but also involves inward attitudes. C.S. Lewis was heard to paraphrase the words of Jesus when he said, "He that but looketh on a plate of ham and eggs to lust after it, hath already committed breakfast with it in his heart."

  That doesn't mean you work at clearing your mind of all possible thoughts. That would be like saying to yourself, "I am not going to think of the word 'corn'." Such an exercise would have exactly the opposite results.

  Paul alludes to this in Romans 8:7-8 where he takes the example of coveting. He says, *"I would not have known about coveting if the Law had not said, 'You shall not covet.' But sin, taking opportunity through the commandment, produced in me coveting of every kind."*

  Instead of focusing entirely upon that which we are to avoid, we are called in the Scriptures to fill our mind with God's thoughts.

Finally, brethren, whatever is true, whatever is honorable, whatever is right, whatever is pure, whatever is lovely, whatever is of good repute, if there is any excellence and if anything worthy of praise, let your mind dwell on these things. (Philippians 4:8).

• Avoid your areas of weakness.

Temptation is tempting. Satan makes it that way. He is intentionally enticing. He baits his hook with the juiciest morsel. When you go fishing, you don't just throw a bare hook into the water. Fish are not tempted by naked hooks. They are enticed by a fat, juicy worm. What is your worm? What is it that entices you? That is the spot where Satan is going to come at you.

> Temptation is like a stray cat. If you feed him he will come back with all of his friends.

The night is almost gone, and the day is at hand. Let us therefore lay aside the deeds of darkness and put on the armor of light. Let us behave properly as in the day, not in carousing and drunkenness, not in sexual promiscuity and sensuality, not in strife and jealousy. But put on the Lord Jesus Christ, and make no provision for the flesh in regard to its lusts. (Romans 13:12-14).

Notice the last injunction. It is that you make no provision for the flesh in regard to its lusts. That means that you look for ways to make sin inconvenient.

- Pray. Jesus taught His disciples to pray that they would not be led into temptation (Matthew 6:13). He also warned His disciples on the night of His betrayal, *"Keep watching and praying, that you may not enter into temptation; the spirit is willing, but the flesh is weak"* (Matthew 26:41).

I have spent an entire career in extinguishing fires and am well acquainted with all sorts of extinguishment tactics. The easiest and most effective method of extinguishing a fire is to not allow it to be ignited in the first place. In the same way, there is a great blessing pronounced upon those who resist temptation.

Blessed is a man who perseveres under trial; for once he has been approved, he will receive the crown of life, which the Lord has promised to those who love Him (James 1:12).

Facing the Flame of Suffering

Beloved, do not be surprised at the fiery ordeal among you, which comes upon you for your testing, as though some strange thing were happening to you. (1 Peter 4:12).

I love Tony Campollo's little book entitled, "The Kingdom of God is a Party." He reminds us that Christians have great cause for rejoicing. Peter does the same thing in his first epistle. That in itself is rather astounding because the situation in which his readers found themselves did not appear to be a cause for rejoicing. They were going through some difficult times. Furthermore Peter does not tell them to rejoice in spite of the circumstances. Instead he tells them to rejoice because of their circumstances.

In this you greatly rejoice, even
though now for a little while, if
necessary, you have been distressed
by various trials (1 Peter 1:6).

Though the translators of the New American
Standard Version have done a good job of
translating this passage, it can appear at first
glance as though they are indicating that suffering
is optional. That isn't the case. Peter uses a
conditional clause in the tiny word "if" that makes
it sound as though this suffering is merely
hypothetical. But the Greek text is worded in
such a way to indicate that the condition is actual
("if it is necessary and it is!").

The recipients of Peter's epistle were going
through some difficult times. There was an
emperor on the throne of the Roman Empire by
the name of Nero. He had set his mind on
persecuting the growing ranks of Christians.
You've heard the old adage, "When in Rome, do
as the Romans." It also applied in this situation:
"When in the Roman Empire, do as the Roman
Emperor." Others were starting to jump on the
persecution bandwagon so that it was no longer
confined to Rome or even the Italian peninsula.

This passage tells me something about trials.
They are necessary. They will take place. They
are unavoidable. Jesus said that in this life you
will have tribulation (John 16:33). Yet in this
middle of such trials, there is a place of rejoicing.
Why? There are several reasons.

First, this passage tells me that I can rejoice

because trials are temporary. Peter says that it is only *now for a little while* that we are distressed by various trials. There is coming a day when the time of trials will be over. There is an end in sight. There is a light at the end of the tunnel and it isn't an oncoming locomotive.

Every career fire fighter knows what it is like to be a rookie. We all started that way. The first year in a fire fighter's life is spent getting through his probationary period. There is material to be learned and skills to be honed and there is usually a certain amount of hazing that comes with the territory. The good news is that it is only temporary. The time of probation eventually comes to an end and the one who has "stuck it out" soon finds that he has overcome and passed to the next stage of his career.

There is a sense in which the trials of this life are like that first year of a fire fighter. Our time on earth is limited and eternity awaits. We live today in what C. S. Lewis called the Shadowlands. The trials of this life will one day fall behind us and then our real life will begin.

Another reason I am able to rejoice in the midst of trials is as I realize that such trials produce a positive result in my life. One of those results is a tested faith.

> *...that the proof of your faith, being more precious than gold which is perishable, even though tested by fire, may be found to result in praise and glory and honor at the revelation*

of Jesus Christ (1 Peter 1:7).

There comes a time in the life of every fire fighter when he faces the flames. That baptism of fire becomes his first test. Will he do the job for which he was trained? Will the faith of his team be affirmed? It is only after coming through the fire that a fire fighter can be known for what he is.

There is a sense in which we, as Christians, are also called to "face the flame." There comes a time when our faith comes under fire and when it is tested by either difficulty or uncertainty or even by doubt. How we handle such adversities test our faith. If our faith is genuine, it will be proven when "the heat is on."

The result of a tested faith is that you can rejoice. You can rejoice because of the secure knowledge that it has seen you through the times of crisis and that it will continue to see you to the end.

Thirdly, I am able to rejoice because what you see is not what you get. Peter goes on to point this out in verses 8 and 9.

> *...and though you have not seen Him, you love Him, and though you do not see Him now, but believe in Him, you greatly rejoice with joy inexpressible and full of glory, obtaining as the outcome of your faith the salvation of your souls. (1 Peter 1:8-9).*

We have a saying that is close to becoming a truism in our culture: "What you see is what you get." It is reflective of the material-minded society in which we live. Fortunately it is a truism that is not true. Peter teaches us that what you see is not necessarily what you get.

That is a good thing because there are a number of things we don't see today. I have been a Christian for a very long time, but I have yet to lay eyes upon Jesus. I believe in Him without ever having seen Him.

Jesus spoke about that kind of faith. It was on the instance when He appeared to Thomas. The first time that Jesus appeared in the Upper Room following His resurrection, Thomas had been out buying hamburgers. He came back to find ten disciples in an uproar. They claimed that they had seen Jesus. But he wasn't buying it. He knew that dead people do not normally make post-death appearances and he determined that he would not believe the report without personal, measurable, experiential evidence. It was a week later when that evidence appeared before him. Suddenly Jesus was there and Doubting Thomas became Believing Thomas.

> *Jesus said to him, "Because you have seen Me, have you believed? Blessed are they who did not see, and yet believed." (John 20:29).*

Do you see it? Jesus was talking about US! He was talking about all those Christians who would come later and who would believe without ever having laid eyes on the risen Lord.

Facing the Flame
of the Tongue

The tongue is a small part of the body, and yet it boasts of great things. Behold, how great a forest is set aflame by such a small fire! (James 3:2-5).

It doesn't take a lot to start a raging fire. Even a little fire can grow into a raging conflagration. Tradition has it that the great Chicago fire was started by a mule kicking over a lantern. Huge forest fires have begun with a careless cigarette. In the same way, the Bible teaches us that our words can serve as both the spark and the kindling that set off a raging inferno.

Though I've spent most of my career in the area of suppression -- those are the guys who come in the big red trucks and put out the fires -- I also hold a fire inspector certification. Fire inspectors have a very different role in the fire department. Their role is not as glamorous. They don't get the news coverage and they don't have their picture in the paper. But they are equally adept at dealing with tragedy. Indeed, it could be argued that they are even more effective than the suppression crews who respond to emergencies. It is the fire inspectors who seek to stop fires before they even start. That is what is described here in the third chapter of James.

If anyone does not stumble in what he says, he is a perfect man, able to bridle the whole body as well (3:2).

James uses the present tense as he describes this status of "not stumbling." This is significant. He is not necessarily saying that the Christian will reach a plateau in which he never stumbles. Rather he is speaking about a habit of life. The mature Christian is one who is not continually stumbling over his tongue. He does not have a "foot-shaped mouth."

Why is it so important to control the tongue? After all, aren't deeds more important than words? Not necessarily. Words often lead to deeds. James illustrates this in two ways:

First is the Illustration of a Horse: *Now if we put the bits into the horses' mouths so that they may obey us, we direct their entire body as well (James 3:3).*

When I was a lot younger, our family used to vacation on my grandfather's farm in the Ozarks. He and my aunts had several horses and we used to ride them upon occasion. Once I tried to ride a horse without the use of a bridle. I jumped onto his back and away he went. That was the first and only time I ever tried that. I found that I had absolutely no say in the matter as to where we were going. The horse immediately headed toward a tree with a low, overhanging branch. I ended up in the branch instead of on the horse. That horse would have never been able to accomplish that maneuver if it had a bit and bridle. I would have been the one in control.

Here is the point. In the same way that a bridle controls a horse, so also the tongue controls the body. It doesn't take much. Just a slip of the tongue. Before you know it, your body is following.

The second illustration found in this passage is of a Ship: *Behold, the ships also, though they are so great and are driven by strong winds, are still directed by a very small rudder, wherever the inclination of the pilot desires. So also the tongue is a small part of the body, and yet it boasts of great things (James 3:4-5).*

A ship is a very ponderous affair. It is so big that it would seem impossible to maneuver. And yet, one man is able to steer a huge ocean liner without even breaking a sweat. How can this be? It is because a huge ship is directed by a relatively tiny machine called a rudder. If James were writing today, he might have said, "Behold, the 747, a huge plane that is controlled by a single lever. In the same way, your body is directed by an organ that weighs only a few ounces -- the tongue.

> *Behold, how great a forest is set aflame by such a small fire! (3:5).*

Most forest fires begin with a single match. Thousands of trees are destroyed by the spark of a single tiny splinter of wood. In the same way, a single careless word can cause enormous damage. You've heard someone say, "I don't hold my feelings in. I just explode and then it's over with." The same can be said of a nuclear bomb and the result is about as devastating. It is like the little rhyme that says:

> *Sticks and stones may break my bones,*
> *But words will flat destroy me.*

Yet the warning of James does not refer only to words spoken in anger. We have already looked at the proverb that speaks of the danger of words spoken in jest, of idle gossip and of the contentious man.

> *Like a madman who throws firebrands, arrows and death,*
> *So is the man who deceives his neighbor,*

And says, "Was I not joking?"
For lack of wood the fire goes out,
And where there is no whisperer,
contention quiets down.
Like charcoal to hot embers and wood
to fire,
So is a contentious man to kindle
strife. (Proverbs 26:18-21).

The proverb describes three different types of men in this passage and they are all bad. The one thing they all have in common is that their words stir up hurt feelings and strife and contention. That is the lesson James brings to us. It is the lesson that words can hurt and they can burn.

> *And the tongue is a fire, the very world of iniquity; the tongue is set among our members as that which defiles the entire body, and sets on fire the course of our life, and is set on fire by hell.*
>
> *For every species of beasts and birds, of reptiles and creatures of the sea, is tamed, and has been tamed by the human race. But no one can tame the tongue; it is a restless evil and full of deadly poison. (James 3:6-8).*

Having shown the power of the tongue as illustrated and compared to a horse's bridle and a ship's rudder, James now moves to his next point -- that the tongue is uncontrollable. The tongue is

71

not bad in itself. It was created by God and is a wonderful thing. The source of the fire described in this passage does not come from the tongue, but from the powers of hell. It is not that the tongue is inherently sinful. It is that it has such a powerful potential. It can do great good. And it can do great evil.

When the tongue is set on fire by hell (that is, when it is used in a sinful way), there are two results. The first result is that it defiles the entire body. Jesus Himself said that it is not that which goes into a man, but that which comes out of a man that defiles him (Matthew 15:11). The point is that you are what you say. The words that you utter are indicative of what you are like on the inside.

The second result is that the tongue sets on fire the course of your life. Your words have a dramatic effect on the course of your life. Many years ago, a preacher asked me, "Do you take this woman to be your lawfully wedded wife?" I only said two words: "I do." My life hasn't been the same since.

James goes on to say that *the tongue...is set on fire by hell (3:6).* The word here translated "hell" is not the normal Greek word for hell. This is the word *Gehenna.* It is not really a Greek word at all. Instead it is a Greek transliteration of the Hebrew word *Ge-honom* – "Valley of Hinnom." It was originally called "The Valley of the sons of Hinnom."

The Valley of Hinnom lay outside the southwest walls of Jerusalem. During the days of

Ahaz and Manasseh in the dark days of Judah's history, human sacrifices were offered there to the pagan god Molech (2 Chronicles 28:3; 33:6).

When Jeremiah was warning Judah of the coming judgment of God against the nation, he said that the Lord would turn the Valley of Hinnom into a valley of slaughter.

> *"For the sons of Judah have done that which is evil in My sight," declares the LORD, "they have set their detestable things in the house which is called by My name, to defile it. And they have built the high places of Topheth, which is in the valley of the son of Hinnom, to burn their sons and their daughters in the fire, which I did not command, and it did not come into My mind.*
>
> *"Therefore, behold, days are coming," declares the LORD, "when it will no more be called Topheth, or the valley of the son of Hinnom, but the valley of the Slaughter; for they will bury in Topheth because there is no other place. And the dead bodies of this people will be food for the birds of the sky, and for the beasts of the earth; and no one will frighten them away." (Jeremiah 7:30-33).*

When Jerusalem fell to the Babylonian invaders during the Old Testament era, there were so many killed that the bodies were dumped into the Valley of Hinnom. In later years, this valley came to be the dumping ground for the refuse of Jerusalem as well as for the bodies of criminals. Fires were kept burning constantly to destroy the rubbish and the filth. It became a place of defilement and continual fire. Because of this, the Valley of Hinnom came to be regarded as a picture of the final punishment of the unrighteous.

When James uses the word *Gehenna*, it refers to all of the filth and the stench of sin that will one day be punished in the Day of Judgment. Jesus said that on that day we will have to give an accounting of all of the words that we have ever said.

> *Either make the tree good, and its fruit good; or make the tree bad, and its fruit bad; for the tree is known by its fruit.*
>
> *You brood of vipers, how can you, being evil, speak what is good? For the mouth speaks out of that which fills the heart. The good man out of his good treasure brings forth what is good; and the evil man out of his evil treasure brings forth what is evil.*
>
> *And I say to you, that every careless word that men shall speak, they shall render account for it in the day of judgment. For by your words you shall be justified, and by your*

words you shall be condemned.
(Matthew 12:33-37).

Jesus said that the reality of what you are comes from the heart. If the heart is good, then it will bear good fruit that will be manifested in good words. The truth of the heart will be manifested in what you do and in what you say.

There is a danger here. It is that you begin to concentrate all of your efforts on cleaning up the outside. But God isn't worried about only cleaning up the externals. He doesn't say, "I want you to be a Christian so we are going to get rid of that habit over there and remove this item over here and then you will be okay." Instead He changes your heart. And if the heart is changed, then after a while the other things begin to change, too.

Being a Christian isn't primarily what you do as much as it is what you are. The corollary to that principle is that what you are will manifest itself in what you do.

Here is the point. You cannot tame the tongue because the tongue merely reflects that which is on the inside. Only God can tame the tongue and He does that by working from the inside out. You go to the Lord and ask Him to change you from the inside out and He will. As a result, you might begin to learn to utilize your tongue in a consistent manner.

With it we bless our Lord and
Father; and with it we curse men, who

75

have been made in the likeness of God; from the same mouth come both blessing and cursing. My brethren, these things ought not to be this way.

Does a fountain send out from the same opening both fresh and bitter water? Can a fig tree, my brethren, produce olives, or a vine produce figs? Neither can salt water produce fresh. (James 3:9-12).

When you come to church and sing praises to the Lord and pray to Him, you are using your tongue to bless His name. And when you leave and get into your car and are driving on the highway and someone cuts you off, you find another use for your tongue. The point is that the two uses are inconsistent with one another.

There is a principle here. It is the principle of *sanctification*. That is a big word, but if you bear with me, I will explain it. When you come to Christ in faith, believing in Him as your Lord and Savior, something extraordinary happens to you. You enter into a process known as sanctification. That is a big word that means that you begin to be set apart from the world and dedicated to the Lord for His special purpose. Your hands are no longer just your hands. They are also His hands. Your tongue is no longer just your tongue. It is now His tongue.

Here is the point. It is inappropriate for a tongue that has been dedicated to the worship of the Lord to be used in the cursing of the Lord's creation.

Imagine driving by a church next Friday evening and you see a great crowd gathered. Wondering what is going on and thinking that you might have slept through the announcements last Sunday, you stop and go inside. There you see that a disc jockey is announcing that mud wrestling will be held in front of the pulpit. What would be your reaction? I hope that you would think it is completely inappropriate. If there is a place for mud wrestling (and I'm not saying that there is), it certainly is not in the place that has been dedicated to the worship of the Lord.

If you are a Christian, then your tongue has been dedicated to the worship of the Lord. To use it for any purpose that does not honor Him is inconsistent. Here is the lesson. When both good and evil come out of the same mouth, one is a lie.

Have you been having trouble with your tongue? Do your words sometimes seem to take on a life of their own? Do you ever catch yourself thinking, "I really wish I had not said that"? Use your tongue. Go to the Lord and confess your sins. He promises that He will hear that prayer of confession and that He, in turn, will speak a word of forgiveness.

Facing the Flame of Judgment

Each man's work will become evident; for the day will show it, because it is to be revealed with fire; and the fire itself will test the quality of each man's work. (1 Corinthians 3:13).

The buildings God didn't want to burn were sprinklered. It is an old saying among fire fighters and it reminds one of the fact that fire preparedness goes a long way. One of the infamous fires of the latter part of the 20th century took place in 1991 in Philadelphia. The fire broke out on the 22nd floor of the 38-story Meridian Bank Building, also known as One

Meridian Plaza.

Instead of calling the fire department, one of the building service workers took the elevator up to the 22nd floor to see if it was a false alarm. When the elevator door opened up on the floor, the smoke and heat were so intense that it drove him to the floor of the elevator. He could not reach up to the elevator buttons to bring the elevator back down.

His calls for help on his mobile radio resulted in the security guard on the ground floor using the automatic override to bring the elevator back down. A second security guard a number of floors above the fire heard this radio transmission and he noticed that the stairways in the building were beginning to fill with smoke. They all made their way downstairs and out of the building. Only then did they realize that they had still not called the fire department.

Shortly after fire fighters arrived at the building, the fire caused an electrical shortage and the entire building was blacked out. This meant the elevators could not be used, even to move equipment. It also meant that all of the hose and air bottles had to be carried up the stairs. The early arriving fire fighters did that, but when they arrived on the floors on which the fire was burning, they found that the water systems were not providing enough water pressure for them to use in their fire attack.

The situation continued to deteriorate and a number of fire fighters encountered doors that were locked, preventing them from escaping when they ran out of air. Before it was over, three fire fighters would lose their lives.

After fighting the fire for 11 hours without success, all fire fighters were pulled out of the building and it was allowed to continue to burn. Floor by floor, the fire continued to make its way upward, it finally reached the 30th floor. This floor had something that had been absent from the lower floors. It had automatic sprinklers. A total of 10 sprinklers activated and put out the fire.

Fire can be terribly destructive. I've seen boats and cars and buildings go up in a matter of minutes. And yet, a bit of planning and preparation can nullify those destructive effects. Here is the principle -- how you build makes a difference in how you face the flames.

Paul uses the analogy of constructing a building when he speaks of how we live our lives and how we do God's work in the world.

> *According to the grace of God which was given to me, as a wise master builder I laid a foundation, and another is building upon it. But let each man be careful how he builds upon it. (1 Corinthians 3:10).*

Paul sees himself as a builder for God's heavenly construction company. He first of all begins with the foundation. This makes sense. After all, you don't try to start construction on a building by laying roof tiles. You don't start with the walls. You always begin the same way. You begin with the foundation.

Paul calls himself a "wise master builder." This is a significant title. It implies that there might be such a thing as a foolish master builder. The phrase "master builder" is translated from the single Greek word from which we get our English word "architect." It points out the fact that some planning ought to go into the building of your life.

You are also a builder. You are either a wise builder or else you are a foolish builder. What is it you are building? You are building your life. How can you tell if it is a good life or a bad life? You can tell the same way that you can tell whether a building contractor has done a good job or a bad job. You can ultimately tell by looking at how the building stands over time.

I have seen some buildings that looked very nice on the outside but which had poor planning and poor foundations so that they did not last. I have also been in some buildings that are over a thousand years old and which are still standing today. What made the difference? It was not just one thing. It was a combination of several factors.

- The foundation.
- The plan.
- The building materials.

Another aspect that we see in the building of a life is that it takes a team. Paul points out that he was not alone in his construction project: *I laid a foundation, and another is building upon it (3:10).*

In the context of this passage, Paul seems to be speaking specifically of building the church. But the same principles that he uses when speaking of building the church also apply to us and the building of our lives. Why do I say that? Because if we are Christians, then we are the building blocks of the church. What is true for the entire church corporately is also usually true of the individual building blocks of the church -- US.

We are not alone in the building of our lives. Because we are people in community, we are co-workers in the building up of one another. The New Testament makes great use of the term "one another."

The people with whom you spend time often have a great impact upon your life. They are the co-laborers with you in building your life. The way the building project goes is impacted by those who do the building. So also, the ones you allow to influence your life have a great deal to say about how your life turns out.

This brings us to a warning. It is a warning to all who build: *But let each man be careful how he builds upon it. (3:10).* We have been applying these words to the way in which you build your house. Paul warns that good building requires due care. You don't just start throwing two by fours together if you want to build a good house. This is a call to live deliberately. You are engaged in God's building project, whether you like it or not. There are only two questions:

- On what foundation are you building?
- What building materials are you using?

When you begin to build a house, there first comes a time of planning, and then you begin to do the actual work. When that work begins, you start from the ground up. You start with the foundation.

> *For no man can lay a foundation other than the one which is laid, which is Jesus Christ. (1 Corinthians 3:11).*

The only foundation of Biblical Christianity is Jesus Christ. He is not merely a part of Christianity. He IS Christianity. Many people seem to think that Christianity is merely a code of morality that says, "Do this" and "Don't do that." Many have tried to hold to these codes without the reality of Jesus Christ. But this will not work. If you are trying to build your life and Jesus Christ is not a major part of that building, then you are building on shifting sand and the entire structure is eventually going to crumble.

The next question you have to ask concerns the building materials. Good building materials are necessary for a sturdy building.

> *Now if any man builds upon the foundation with gold, silver, precious stones, wood, hay, straw, each man's work will become*

evident; for the day will show it, because it is to be revealed with fire; and the fire itself will test the quality of each man's work. (1 Corinthians 3:12-13).

Having secured an adequate foundation in Jesus Christ, the next question that faces the builder is the choice of building materials. Paul describes two basic types.

- Valuable materials: *Gold, silver, precious stones*.
- Inferior materials: *Wood, hay, straw*.

What are the differences between these two categories? The most obvious difference is that one is relatively fire-proof while the other burns very easily. But there is something else. Wood, hay and straw are very easy to come by, especially if you live in an agricultural economy as did Paul's readers. Gold, silver or precious stones are not nearly so commonplace.

What do these materials represent? Do they represent natural abilities? Do they represent spiritual gifts? No. I would suggest that the identity of these building materials cannot be understood apart from the context of the previous two chapters of 1st Corinthians. Throughout these two chapters, Paul has been making a series of contrasts between the believer and the unbeliever.

Unbeliever	Believer
Sees the message of the cross as foolishness	Sees the message of the cross as the power of God
Those who are perishing (1:18).	Those who are being saved (1:18)
Tried to come to know God through its wisdom (1:21)	Came to know God by the preaching of the cross (1:21)
The wisdom of men (2:5)	The wisdom of God (2:5)
The natural man does not accept the things of the Spirit of God (2:14)	But he who is spiritual appraises all things (2:15)
Must have a diet of milk (3:2)	Able to receive solid food (3:2)
Builds with wood, hay and straw	Builds with gold, silver and precious stones

This contrast continues here. The wood, the hay and the straw refer to those things that are built by the natural man. The gold, silver and precious stones are those things that are built by the spiritual man.

Paul has already established that the foundation is Jesus Christ. He is building upon that foundation and others are also building upon that foundation. But not everyone is using the same building materials. Some are using building materials that are of the Spirit. Others are using building materials that are of the flesh.

It is interesting to note that Paul lists three different types of building materials that are used by the Spirit of God. They are gold and silver and precious stones. These are all seen as good things. He does not say that gold is better than silver or that precious stones are not quite up to the proper standards. Yet I think that there is a very specific reason that three different appropriate materials are mentioned. It is because not all of the building materials of the Spirit are the same. There is a lesson here. It is that you can follow the Lord and do His will and yet the practical outworking of that might be very different from someone else who is also following the Lord and doing His will. One person might be called by the Lord to follow Him and do His will in a working environment. Another might be called to be a homemaker. Another might be called to be a missionary in a foreign country.

Here is the principle. Not all of God's work is the same work. Just because one man has a ministry of evangelism does not mean that another is wrong to have a ministry of teaching. What is important is that we are using the proper building materials and that we are building upon the correct foundation.

You are building for eternity. You may object, "But John, I'm not building anything. I'm not an apostle or a prophet or a preacher or a Bible teacher." It doesn't matter. You are still building. The only question is whether you are using the right building materials. You are either building with gold, silver and precious stones or else you are building with wood, hay and straw.

This is the problem. It is possible for the Christian to use the wrong building materials. It is possible for the Christian to build with the building materials of the flesh. It is possible for the Christian to act like the unbeliever.

This is dangerous. It is dangerous because there is coming a time of judgment. It is dangerous because there is coming a time when the Heavenly Building Inspector of the universe will pass judgment on the quality of your work.

> *...each man's work will become evident; for the day will show it, because it is to be revealed with fire; and the fire itself will test the quality of each man's work. (1 Corinthians 3:13).*

A new building usually must pass an official inspection before a certificate of occupancy can be issued. Government officials come out to the site of the building and test its structure to make sure that it is built according to the proper codes. This is to insure that the building is sound.

God also has a set of standards by which He will judge the quality of our labors. There is coming a day of judgment.

> *For we must all appear before*

*the judgment seat of Christ, that
each one may be recompensed for
his deeds in the body, according to
what he has done, whether good
or bad. (2 Corinthians 5:10).*

There are several observations that we
ought to make from this passage. First, notice
that no one is exempt from this judgment. Paul
says that we must all appear before the judgment
seat of Christ. The purpose of the judgment is to
recompense each one for his deeds in the body.
This judgment is action-oriented. This will be a
judgment that looks back at the actions you took
while you were in the body.

At this point, you might object, "I thought
that God judges the heart." Indeed He does. But
your outward actions always come forth as the
fruit of what is in your heart.

Don't miss this! The way you live is a
direct result of what you believe. Don't tell me
that you love Jesus if you do not obey His
commandments. Show me your faith by your
works and they I will know that it is true faith.

Notice also that this judgment will include
everything that you have done, both the good and
the bad. Nothing is going to be hidden. It will all
be brought out into the open. I was working with
the fire department when Hurricane Andrew
swept across South Florida in 1992. I had
opportunity to go down to where the greatest
damage had been done by that great storm. There
were hundreds of houses that had been completely

blown away. Entire communities were gone. But in the very center of the worst devastation, I noted one house that was virtually untouched. It was a house made of coral rock. It had weathered the storm. It had been tested and the storm had not been able to hurt it.

There is a storm warning. A storm of testing is on the horizon. It shall come and it shall test the building of your life. You will be tested to see of what it is you are made.

> *Each man's work will become evident; for the day will show it* (3:13).

Your work is not evident today. I can look at the things that you do and I cannot always be certain whether they are of the Spirit or of the flesh. But there is coming a day when such uncertainty will vanish away. There is coming a day when the true character of your life will be known. It is the day of judgment. It is the day when Christ shall return. The means of that testing will be through fire.

> *It is to be revealed with fire; and the fire itself will test the quality of each man's work* (3:13).

Fire is used throughout the Bible as a symbol of judgment. God rained down fire from heaven on the wicked cities of Sodom and Gomorrah (Genesis 19:24). The sacrifices that were made in the tabernacle were to be burned with fire (Leviticus 1:7; 2:2; 3:3; 4:12). Joshua ordered that Jericho be burnt to the ground and, when Achan stole some of its plunder, he and his family and all of their possessions were burned with fire (Joshua 6:24; 7:15). John the Baptist warned that the coming Messiah would baptize in the Spirit and in fire (Matthew 3:11). Jesus told the parable of the wheat and the tares and how those who had been planted by the enemy would be gathered into the furnace of fire (Matthew 13:42). Paul said that Jesus shall be revealed from heaven with His mighty angels in flaming fire (2 Thessalonians 1:7).

Now Paul tells us that the fire will actually be the means by which our works shall be judged. They will have to stand up to a trial by fire. This fire will not harm gold or silver or precious stones. The only thing that fire will do to such materials is to purify them.

> *If any man's work which he has built upon it remains, he shall receive a reward. If any man's work is burned up, he shall suffer loss; but he himself shall be saved, yet so as through fire.*
>
> *Do you not know that you are a temple of God, and that the Spirit of God dwells in you? If any man destroys the temple of God, God will destroy him, for the temple of God is holy, and that is what you are. (1 Corinthians 3:14-*

17).

Paul describes three types of laborers in this passage. They are as follows:

- The man whose work remains (3:14).
- The man whose work is burned up (3:15).
- The man who destroys the temple of God (3:17).

1. The Man Whose Work Remains: *If any man's work which he has built upon it remains, he shall receive a reward* (3:14).

   This is the first type of laborer. He is the laborer who is faithful to the Master. He is the laborer who builds on the proper foundation and who uses the proper building materials. God rewards this faithful laborer.

2. The Man Whose Work Is Burned up: *If any man's work is burned up, he shall suffer loss; but he himself shall be saved, yet so as through fire* (3:15).

   This is the second type of laborer. His work is on the proper foundation, but it is of the wrong materials. He is a believer in Christ and is rooted on the foundation of salvation, but his life and his work has too often resembled that of the unbeliever. As a result, he suffers loss. His life's work has been wasted. It is burned up.

Yet God is gracious. This unfaithful laborer is still saved, though all that for which he has worked has been lost to the flames of judgment. He did not deserve to be saved (none of us did). But God does not give him what he deserves. God gives him grace. God never gives any of us what we deserve. If He did, we would be in hell right now.

3. The Man Who Destroys the Temple of God: *If any man destroys the temple of God, God will destroy him* (3:17).

Here is the third type of individual. He is the man who attempts to destroy the temple of God. He is not a faithful laborer. He is not even an unfaithful laborer. He is an enemy. He is one who attempts to tear down rather than to build. He is one who tries to divide rather than to promote unity. He is one who is more interested in holding up the distinctions between Paul and Peter and Apollos than in building the kingdom of Christ.

What is this "temple of God" that he tries to destroy? It is the church. We see this in the previous verse. Paul says that *you are a temple of God and that the Spirit of God dwells in you* (3:16).

That is a striking description. It is one that is reminiscent of the temple in Jerusalem. The temple was the place where God's presence had once been manifested. It signified the presence of God on earth.

Within the innermost part of the temple had been a special treasure. The ark of the covenant. This was a wooden chest overlaid with gold. Inside had been kept the pieces of the ten commandments. On the top of the ark was a golden cover known as the mercy seat. The statues of two cherubim spread their wings over the mercy seat. This mercy seat was the royal throne of God. It was the most holy place on earth.

But there is another holy place today. It is the church. I do not mean that it is a building. The church is not a building. The church is the body of believers. This is the most holy place of God. The Spirit of God dwells inside the heart of each and every believer and within the church collectively.

Are you a believer? Are you one of God's people? If so, then the Spirit of God lives inside you. You are God's holy place on earth. You need to remember that. You need to be aware that you are God's place of holiness in the midst of an impure world.

God takes very special care of His holy place. He says that if any man destroys that holy place, then God will destroy him. This is serious. The day of judgment is coming. In light of that truth, you need to ask yourself where you stand. What kind of laborer are you?

Facing the Flame of Religion

What therefore you worship in ignorance, this I proclaim to you (Acts 17:23).

Fighting a fire on a passenger ship has been likened to dealing with a fire in a high rise building. One obvious difference is that ships sink. I've yet to see a building do that.

Passenger ships have come a long way in the realm of fire safety. The newer ships are all sprinklered and have all sorts of backup systems, making them as safe as possible. That hasn't always been the case. From our perspective, the most hazardous of the ships were the smaller day cruisers. These were the vessels that would take a group of gamblers out past the 12-mile limit and anchor for a few hours before coming back into Port.

The alarm went off one morning and the call came in that a fire was underway aboard one such passenger ship that was loaded with people and ready to sail. The cause of the fire was a study in irony. A couple of United States Coast Guard officers had come aboard to test the crews for a fire drill and were putting those crews through their paces, sounding the test alarms. One of the cooks had just turned on the deep fat fryer in a galley when he heard the alarm, so he left to find his fire station. The drill was still underway when thick, black smoke began to billow out of the galley.

We received the alarm and responded to the dock where the ship was still moored. I was driving a command vehicle and, as I rolled up on the dock, I could see the black smoke and water streams all over the ship as inexperienced crews continued to shoot water at the smoke.

In those days, I was running two fire engines but only had an officer on one of them. That left me an officer short. Because of this, I established command over the radio and called for backup, and then went with the initial crew to see for myself how extensive was the fire. If it could not be extinguished in the next five to ten minutes, then I would have to come back down and set up a regular command post from which to run all of the different sectors, groups and divisions that would be established.

One engine was ordered to get water. My

lieutenant would oversee that operation. I grabbed a rope bag from one of the engines and called for the remaining crew to grab a couple of high-rise packs and to follow me up onto the ship. We made entry through the crew's gangway and only paused for a second while I grabbed an adaptor from the ship's gear locker.

Then we were hoofing it up the stairs until we had gotten to the deck where the fire was located. We must have been on an adrenalin high because no one paused for a breath even though we were weighed down with gear. We made our way aft to a point where the smoke seemed to have the greatest density. We found ourselves on the narrow deck just outside the aft galley.

Here I met with the ship's first officer. He and his fire crews had attempted to fight the fire with dry chem extinguishers, but had been pushed out by the heavy heat and smoke. There was a small mountain of spent extinguishers that bore testimony to their failure. The ship's fire doors had been closed automatically from the bridge to prevent the fire and smoke from traveling through the rest of the ship. There were passengers both forward and aft and these numbered in the hundreds. Evacuation had started, but would progressively become more difficult if we did not extinguish the fire immediately.

While the attack crew used the adaptor I had provided to connect their attack line to the ship's standpipe system, I secured a rope to the railing and dropped the other end forty feet to the dock below where the Engine crew was wrestling their hard suction hose into place so that they could draw an unlimited supply of water from the ocean. They secured one end of a 3-inch hoseline to my rope and I had a fire fighter pull it up and secure it to provide an alternate source of water should we need it.

By this time, my attack team had their hoseline ready. They moved into the interior of the ship, pushing through a compartment and then through another door to come to the room where the fire had originated. Using an indirect attack, they banked their hosestream off the ceiling, allowing the heat of the fire to turn it to steam and thereby smother the seat of the fire. Within a minute or two, the fire had been darkened and it was only left to check for possible extension to see if the fire had spread to previously unaffected areas.

By the time units from Fort Lauderdale and the had County arrived, the fire was out and there was nothing more to be done except for mopping up operations. Thanks to speedy action, a crisis was averted without a single injury.

Further investigation revealed that the ship's crew had tried to extinguish the fire on their own instead of calling for the fire department. The small mountain of spent extinguishers we passed on the way to the fire stood as mute testimony to their lack of effectiveness. It wasn't that they hadn't put forth the effort. It was simply that they were untrained. They were trying to do something for which they lacked the training.

Religion has a way of calling us to do the same thing. Lots of activity and little results. Paul saw this when he came to Athens.

> *Now while Paul was waiting for them at Athens, his spirit was being provoked within him as he was observing the city full of idols. (Acts 17:16).*

Athens was a thoroughly pagan city. The crown of the city was its Parthenon, dedicated to the city's namesake, the goddess Athena. Even today, people flock from all over the world to see the ruins of the Parthenon, to gaze at its magnificent columns.

Paul had come to Athens for a breather. He was on vacation. He was sightseeing like a good tourist. But the sights included all manners of idols. Pliny says that there were over 30,000 idols in Athens during this time in history. It was a saying that it was easier to find a god in Athens than it was to find a man.

Paul sees this gross idolatry. He sees the temples to all of the pagan deities. He sees the cultic sensual worship. He sees a city going to hell. At this point, he could no longer be silent. He is constrained to speak.

Are you provoked by sin? Does it provoke you to speak out? As we live in an increasingly pagan society, a danger that we face is that we are no longer provoked by sin. It no longer repels us. It becomes a part of our social background and, like a shot of spiritual Novocain; we become deadened to its effects.

I have seen death a number of times in my career as a fire fighter. It is a part of my job. And to a certain extent, I think that I have become a bit hardened to it. Exposure leads to hardening.

How can we combat this deadening process? By becoming alive to the gospel and tender to the Scriptures which set it forth. By coming to the cross and embracing it through faith. By believing the gospel each day. That was the message that Paul began to share with the people of Athens.

> *So he was reasoning in the synagogue with the Jews and the God-fearing Gentiles, and in the market place every day with those who happened to be present. (Acts 17:17).*

Paul comes to Athens and he doesn't know a soul in the entire city. There isn't a Christian to be found anywhere. Is that bad? No, it's good because it means that there are plenty of opportunities for harvest.

It is like the story of the two shoe salesmen that went to a community in the interior of Africa. One wrote back, "I am coming home as there is no market for our product. No one wears shoes here." The other salesman wrote back, "Send more shoes; there is a tremendous opportunity for sales. No one wears shoes here yet!" Paul looked at this pagan city and he saw opportunity.

As was his custom, he first directed his attention to the synagogue. Why did he do this? It is because they already had a knowledge of God's word and they could build upon their faith.

But Paul didn't limit his evangelistic efforts to once a week or to the locale of the synagogue. His Christianity did not stay within the four walls of the church. He took it out into the marketplace.

Do you have a marketplace faith? Or do you keep your faith safely tucked away to be brought out only when you come to church? Paul had a very simple strategy of evangelism. Anyone who happened to be around him was evangelized. He was always talking about the gospel and if you found yourself within earshot of Paul, then you could not help but to hear the gospel.

What do people hear when they are around you? They hear whatever it is about which you are passionate. If you love fishing, then they hear about fish. If you love sports, then that will be the thing they hear from you. Go to God and ask Him for a passion for the Lord. And then speak out from your passion.

> *And also some of the Epicurean and Stoic philosophers were conversing with him. Some were saying, "What would this idle babbler wish to say?"*

Others, "He seems to be a proclaimer of strange deities," -- because he was preaching Jesus and the resurrection. (Acts 17:18).

There are two philosophical groups mentioned here who had dealings with Paul in Athens. The first of these were the Epicureans. Epicurus founded a school in Athens in 300 B.C. He taught that there are no gods. His philosophy was that of 1 Corinthians 15:32 - "Let us eat and drink, for tomorrow we die." They denied a future judgment or even that God has a hand in any present actions. There is no afterlife and when you are dead, you are dead so enjoy the present.

The other group were the Stoics. They taught that god is everywhere and that the world is under an impersonal force of natural law. When we die, we are absorbed back into the divine.

The Epicureans said: "Enjoy life!"
The Stoics said: "Endure life!"
Paul is going to tell them how to obtain life.

These two philosophies are diametrically opposed. But they do agree on one thing. They both agree that they are opposed to the message of the gospel. What is it about the gospel that they are opposed? Both of these philosophies agreed on several points.

- There is no personal God.
- There is no purpose in life.
- There is no such thing as a resurrection from the dead.

Here is Paul preaching of a personal Messiah who has come and who has died for sins and who has risen from the dead and who promises that those who believe will one day rise as well.

They resort to name-calling. Whenever someone resorts to name-calling, you can realize that they have no better argument to offer. They call Paul a *idle babbler* -- literally, a "seed picker." It describes one who would pick bits and pieces from different philosophies.

I've been involved in plenty of firehouse arguments. You can always tell when someone is losing the argument -- he stops giving reasons and he shifts to name-calling.

> *And they took him and brought him to the Areopagus, saying, "May we know what this new teaching is which you are proclaiming? For you are bringing some strange things to our ears; so we want to know what these things mean."*
> *Now all the Athenians and the strangers visiting there used to spend their time in nothing other than telling or hearing something*

new. *(Acts 17:19-21).*

The place to which they brought Paul was known as the "Areopagus." This comes from two Greek words. *Ares* was the Greek god of war; known to the Romans as Mars. *Pagus* is Greek for "hill." This is why some translations refer to this as "Mars Hill." But it was more than merely a place named after a Greek war god. The Areopagus was connected to the Acropolis of Athens by a narrow ridge. On the top of this hill was the traditional meeting place for the judicial body of Athens. We would call it "capitol hill." Unfortunately for the Athenians, they were no longer in charge of their own government. Like most of the rest of the known world, they were under the rulership of Rome. And so, the Areopagus had become a meeting place for discussion regarding philosophy.

> *So Paul stood in the midst of the Areopagus and said, "Men of Athens, I observe that you are very religious in all respects.*
>
> *"For while I was passing through and examining the objects of your worship, I also found an altar with this inscription, 'TO AN UNKNOWN GOD.' Therefore what you worship in ignorance, this I proclaim to you. (Acts 17:22-23).*

Paul does not immediately begin talking about Jesus. Neither does he quote from the Old Testament or appeal to the Jewish prophets. Instead he starts where they are. He starts with something to which they can relate. He points to one of their pagan altars.

Greek tradition had it that a mysterious plague once swept through the city of Athens. All sorts of cures were attempted and nothing worked. The people assumed that one of the city's many gods had been offended. But which one? There were thousands of pagan deities. Athens was the god capital of the world.

The citizens called in a consultant; a prophet from the island of Crete. His name was Epimenides. He concluded that the plague was the handiwork of some unknown god which had been offended.

Epimenides ordered that a flock of hungry sheep be turned loose on the Areopagus. They watched the sheep and whenever any one of the sheep would lie down and not eat, an altar was erected on that spot and the sheep was sacrificed to the unknown god. Presumably there were a number of such altars which had been built.

It was now many hundreds of years later, but there still remained at least one such altar to the unknown god. We do not know for certain that it dated all the way back to the time of Epimenides, but its distinction was the same. And it is to this altar that Paul now directs the attention of his hearers.

"You Athenians have been worshiping at

one particular altar who is known as the UNKNOWN GOD. Let me tell you about Him."

There are a lot of wrong perceptions about God today. They border on downright paganism. Some see Him as the impersonal force from Star Wars. He is described as the "higher power" of alcoholics anonymous. Still others speak of Him as the "man upstairs." These are all inadequate to describe the God who is there. But instead of walking up to someone and calling them a pagan, how about introducing them to the God in whom they claim to believe?

Paul answers both the Epicureans as well as the Stoics. First, they deny a personal God -- He shows them the God who is both personal and yet who transcends the little petty gods of the Greek pantheon.

> *"The God who made the world and all things in it, since He is Lord of heaven and earth, does not dwell in temples made with hands; nor is He served by human hands, as though He needed anything, since He Himself gives to all people life and breath and all things (Hebrews 17:24-25).*

These two philosophies had rejected the idea of the little petty gods that were worshiped by the Greeks – Gods who had all of the frailties of humans. Paul says, "You are right! God isn't like that at all." He is the Creator of the world and doesn't need your little temples.

Secondly, they deny human purpose – He demonstrates how that God's ordination of man's life gives him a unique and special purpose.

> *And He made from one man every nation of mankind to live on all the face of the earth, having determined their appointed times and the boundaries of their habitation, that they would seek God, if perhaps they might grope for Him and find Him, though He is not far from each one of us; for in Him we live and move and exist, as even some of your own poets have said, 'For we also are His children.'" (Acts 17:26-27).*

Do you see what Paul presents to these pagan unbelievers? It is the message of a sovereign God who has ordained all things under the sun. But it is not just the transcendence of God which is presented. It is also the nearness of God which is seen. God is both the God of all the universe as well as being a personal God who listens to your individual prayers. These are held in tension.

Transcendence	*Immanence*
Creator (He made from one man every nation) and sovereign determiner...	...that they would seek God, though He is not far from each one of us.

They rejected the small petty gods of Greece and so did Paul. He cites their own pagan poets to get them to see that even their own culture affirms the idea that God is there. Two poets are cited: *Some of your poets have said* (17:28).

There are several different ancient poets who had made these quotes. None of them were believers. None of them worshiped the God of Abraham and Isaac and Jacob. How can Paul use these quotes? Paul believes that the reason for these quotes and the false religions to which they hold is the misapplied light of natural revelation. He is not saying that they know God. Indeed, he started his entire sermon with the recognition that they did not know Him and that they even showed a realization that they did not know Him by having an altar to the UNKNOWN GOD.

Are these poets cited in lieu of citing Old Testament Scripture? No. These poets were talking about Zeus in the context of their writings. Paul only quotes them as illustrative.

> *"Being then the children of God, we ought not to think that the Divine Nature is like gold or silver or stone, an image formed by the art and thought of man. (Acts 17:29).*

Do you see the point of the argument? We are people. We have "person-ness." And if we have personality, then it only follows that the One

110

who created up also has personality. That is why any view of God as merely an impersonal force must of necessity be wrong. Impersonal cannot create personal. That is what is wrong with evolutionary philosophy. It can make all sorts of theories, but it cannot explain how the impersonal can create the personal.

> *"Therefore having overlooked the times of ignorance, God is now declaring to men that all people everywhere should repent, because He has fixed a day in which He will judge the world in righteousness through a Man whom He has appointed, having furnished proof to all men by raising Him from the dead." (Acts 17:30-31).*

Verse 30 says that God has *"overlooked the times of ignorance."* What does this mean? The same idea is taught in Acts 14:16 were God *"permitted all the nations to go their own ways."*

Something wonderful happened when the church began. There was an evangelism explosion and it sent the gospel throughout the entire world. Prior to this time, if you wanted to hear the gospel you had to come to Israel. But now the gospel came to you.

That brings a tremendous responsibility. It is a responsibility to repent - to turn to God and to be saved. There are three things that underscore this need for repentance.

The first is that there is an inescapable day coming. God has fixed a day when he will judge the world. Everyone knows this. You know it, don't you? You know there is a day coming when your life is going to be laid open before everyone, and all the value of it, or the lack of value, will be evident. There is coming a day when every life will be evaluated.

Secondly, we see that there is an unchallengeable Judge. The One who will do the evaluating will not be a god, remote upon Mount Olympus, but he will be a Man, someone who has lived right here with us, who knows what human life is like, who has felt everything we feel. He will be the One who passes judgment on that day.

Finally, we learn that God has given us the evidence of the resurrection. I believe this to be the ultimate apologetic. God took a dead man and made Him alive. This is where Christianity ultimately rests. If you can disprove the resurrection of Jesus, you can destroy Christianity in one blow. But as long as that fact remains unshaken and undestroyed, Christianity is indestructible. It rests upon that one great demonstrable fact -- that God raised Jesus from the dead. That is the guarantee that all God says *will happen.*

Now when they heard of the resurrection of the dead, some began to sneer, but others said, "We shall hear you again concerning this."

So Paul went out of their midst. But some men joined him and believed, among whom also were Dionysius the Areopagite and a woman named Damaris and others with them. (Acts 17:32-34).

There are always one of three reactions to the gospel. When people hear they will initially do one of three things.

- Rejection: *Some began to sneer*
- Reluctance: *Others said, "We shall hear you again concerning this."*
- Repentance: *Some men joined him and believed*

There is initially one of three reactions to the gospel. But eventually there are only two possible reactions. Reluctance does one of two things. It moves either in one direction or the other. Every time you hear the message of the gospel, your heart is moved in one of these two directions. Which way is your heart moving today?

Facing the Flame of the Future

The end of all things is at hand (1 Peter 4:7).

I've served as a fire fighter for over 25 years. I came up through the ranks from lieutenant to captain to battalion chief. It has been a good and rewarding career. I was allowed to play with all sorts of high-tech toys and gadgets, and to lead a committed group of professional men and women to perform a community service by responding to emergencies and saving lives and property.

There have been those times, especially when I've been on my hands and knees in pitch black smoke in the bowels of a ship where I have

115

asked myself, "Why on earth am I doing this?" But over all, it has been a career that has been financially rewarding and which has been fulfilling in every sense of the word.

Because it is a hazardous profession -- a young man's profession -- it has built into it the potential for an early retirement. When one reaches that stage, you can retire and stay home and they will mail you your retirement check each month. In 2003, I crossed that imaginary line so that I am now eligible to retire. After that time, I began to notice an interesting phenomenon. There was an extra bounce to my step. I had always enjoyed my job, but that enjoyment factor move up a couple of degrees. There was a sense of anticipation that new things were on the horizon.

I was asked on a number of occasions, "When are you going to do it? When are you going to retire?" And my answer was usually short of profound: "I don't know. As long as I want to. As long as I'm still enjoying it. It could be this month. Or it could be a few months from now. But it will be soon."

Peter says much the same thing in his first epistle. He says in 1 Peter 4:7 that *the end of all things is at hand*." Commentators and Bible scholars have wondered what things he might have been talking about.

- Peter might have been talking about the end of his own life. We know from church tradition that he was put

116

to death at the orders of Emperor Nero as a part of the Roman persecutions of the church. Within this same chapter, Peter will go on to speak of the fiery ordeal that Christians are facing in his day (4:12).

- He might have been speaking of the end of the Jewish sacrificial system and its temple that would soon be destroyed by the Romans. We know today that this took place in A.D. 70, but as Peter pens these words, that destruction is still on the horizon.

- He might be speaking of literally the end of all things -- the second coming of Christ and the end of human history.

I tend to think that it is all three that are in view and that "all things" literally means "all things." There is a sense in which the coming of Jesus to the earth ushered in the last days and we have been living in the last days ever since.

On the day of Pentecost, Peter was able to stand up and quote Joel's prophecy about how it shall be that in the last days God would pour forth His Spirit upon all mankind and he was able to say, "Look, here it is!"

Peter said in his day and we can still say in our own day that the end of all things is at hand. There are no more prophecies that have to be fulfilled. There are no more signs that have to be seen. There is nothing more on the prophetic agenda that has to be checked off.

The end of all things is at hand. It could end today before you finish reading this book. Or it could be another thousand years. The Bible teaches that no one knows the day or the hour. No one knows when Christ is going to return. And that means His coming is at hand. It could take place at any time.

You have no guarantees on life. If there is one thing that I have learned in all of my years as a fire fighter, it is that things happen unexpectedly. You have no guarantees on how long you are going to live. It could well be that, for some of us today, the end of all things is at hand.

If that is true, and Peter says that it is, then there are some practical implications as to how such a truth ought to impact the way that I live today.

> "Do not look so sad. We shall meet soon again." "Please, Aslan," said Lucy, "what do you call soon?" "I call all times soon," said Aslan; and instantly he was vanished away.
> - C.S. Lewis, Voyage of the Dawn Treader

You see, prophecy in the Bible isn't given merely to satisfy my morbid curiosity. It is not given so that I can draw up all sorts of charts of future history and play the part of a spiritual soothsayer. It is given so that I might be motivated to live in a certain manner today.

Peter says, "The end of all things is at

hand and, because the end of all things is at hand, we ought to live in a certain way." Let's look at it.

First of all, I want you to note that, because the end of all things is at hand, we ought to be serious about prayer

> *The end of all things is at hand; therefore, be of sound judgment and sober spirit for the purpose of prayer (1 Peter 4:7).*

Right at the outset, Peter says that we ought to take prayer more seriously. Why does he say this? Because he knows that we all have a tendency to take prayer too lightly. Jesus pointed this out in the Temple when He took up a scourge against those who had made a mockery of the Temple. He said, "My Father's house is to be a house of prayer."

Jesus didn't do that because there was a complete absence of prayer within the Temple. But somewhere along the line, prayer had ceased to be a priority. It was merely something that was done at the proper time to fill in between the praise and the preaching. As such, it had come to be taken for granted.

How would that change if you thought that today was indeed your last day upon planet earth? If you were told that before the sun set upon this day, you would stand before your Maker, how serious would you be about prayer?

Peter says, "You get serious about prayer

right now because the end of all things IS at hand." You do not know how much longer you have. You are just a heartbeat away from His presence.

Peter calls you to pray. But that is not all. He also tells you how you ought to pray. It is seen in this same verse.

1.   You are to Pray with Sound Judgment: *Be of sound judgment (4:7)*.

How does being of sound judgment affect the way in which you pray? It means that you pray with your eyes open. It means that you pray with purpose and understanding. It means that you pray intelligently.

James tells us that *you do not have because you do not ask. 3 You ask and do not receive, because you ask with wrong motives, so that you may spend it on your pleasures* (James 4:2-3).

We have a problem when we do not ask in the first place. We also have a problem when we ask for the wrong things and when we ask with the wrong attitude.

2.   You are to Pray Seriously: *Be of sound judgment and sober spirit for the purpose of prayer (4:7)*.

How do you pray with sober spirit? It means that you go into prayer with the full

120

realization that you are coming into the presence of the Sovereign King of all the universe. In C.S. Lewis' tale, "The Chronicles of Narnia," Lucy sees Aslan, the Christ-figure after having been parted from him for many a year and exclaims, "Aslan, you're bigger."

"That is because you are older, little one," answered he.

"Not because you are?" she asks.

"I am not. But every year you grow, you will find me bigger."

Here is an interesting truth. The older and more mature you are in the Lord, the bigger you will see that He is.

Secondly, I want you to note that, because the end of all things is at hand, we ought to be fervent in our love

> *Above all, keep fervent in your love for one another, because love covers a multitude of sins. (1 Peter 4:8).*

Notice that this is specifically described as a love that is *for one another*. You would have thought that Peter would have said that we are to be fervent in our love for the Lord. But Peter had been taught something special about love from the Lord.

Do you remember the incident? It took place after the resurrection. Jesus met His disciples by the Sea of Galilee and repeated a miracle of a miraculous catch of fish. It must have seemed a bit like deja vu to the disciples. Several years earlier, they had been with Jesus on a boat in the Sea of Galilee after fishing all night and catching nothing. At His insistence they had lowered their nets into the sea and had pulled them up tight and full of fish. Several years have passed and they are back.

- It is the same Sea of Galilee.
- It is in the same boats
- They are the same disciples.
- They again have fished all night.
- Again they are given instructions about their actions.
- And once again there is a great catch of fish.

After it is all over, they sit with Jesus by the sea as they finish up their meal and Jesus turns to Peter and asks the question: "Do you love me?" Three times the question goes forth and again there is the same sense of deja vu, for Peter had recently been asked on three successive occasions, "Do you know Him? And on three successive occasions Peter had denied His Lord.

But this time it is different. Jesus asks, "Peter, do you love me?" And when Peter answers in the affirmative, Jesus gives a repeated injunction: "Then feed my sheep." Do you see it? Peter is passing on that same command here. Do you love the Lord? Then show it by loving His people. Show it by keeping *fervent in your love for one another.*

The third thing I want you to note from this passage is that, because the end of all things is at hand, we ought to be hospitable toward one another

> *Be hospitable to one another*
> *without complaint. (1 Peter 4:9).*

Hospitality. It isn't a word that we use much within the city. Our English word "hospitality" sounds too much like "hospital" and no one likes to go to a hospital. But the Greek word has a different sound: *Philoxenoi* -- literally "lovers of strangers." Our English language has coined a different word -- "xenophobia" -- a fear of strangers. But the Bible says that we ought to be characterized by a love of strangers.

When you live in a big city, everyone becomes a stranger and it's hard to love everyone. But that it exactly what we are commanded to do. And furthermore, we are called to exercise that hospitality without complaint.

Do you ever complain about the traffic? All of those other people on the road; people you do not know but who are in your way and who are slowing you from getting to your destination. You are called to be hospitable to them and even to that one who cut you off. Peter gets specific in this verse. He says to be hospitable toward one another. That is a family phrase. That brings it here into the church. The church is to be a place of hospitality.

When I think of the quality hospitality, my mind goes back over 30 years ago to an elderly couple in a church where my wife and I eventually served as youth directors. Their names were Mr. and Mrs. Bucksbaum and it was likely on our first or second Sunday to that church that they invited us into their home for a small lunch. I don't recall what they served or what we talked about, but I can remember their hospitality. They loved the Lord and they wanted to share that love with others. So whenever they saw an unfamiliar face in church, they would make it a point to invite that person to their home.

Have you opened your home to strangers who come to the church? Perhaps it could be through the hosting of a small group Bible study. Or it might be something as simple as inviting a visitor to the church to share in a meal.

Fourthly, I want you to see that, because the end of all things is at hand, we ought to be faithful in our stewardship

> *As each one has received a special gift, employ it in serving one another, as good stewards of the manifold grace of God. Whoever speaks, let him speak, as it were, the utterances of God; whoever serves, let him do so as by the strength which God supplies; so that in all things God may be glorified through Jesus*

Christ, to whom belongs the glory
and dominion forever and ever.
Amen. (1 Peter 4:10-11).

A steward in ancient times was the one who managed a household. More often than not, he was the slave of the master of the house and it was his job to make sure that everything in the house ran properly. The steward did not own the house himself. The care of the house was entrusted to him. We might refer to him as the "housekeeper."

Here is the point. You have been entrusted with being the housekeeper of God's house. What is His house? It is the church. It is the collected and gathered people whom He has called by His name. You are charged with the upkeep and the care and the growth of that body.

You might think, "Wait a minute, isn't that why we pay the pastor and staff? Isn't that their job?" And the answer is no. Their job is to equip you to do your job. That is the principle that is seen in Ephesians 4.

And He gave some as apostles,
and some as prophets, and some
as evangelists, and some as
pastors and teachers, for the
equipping of the saints for the
work of service, to the building up
of the body of Christ (Ephesians
4:11-12).

The same principle is seen here in the words of Peter. He doesn't say, "Go out and hire a senior pastor who will do the work of the ministry while everyone else comes on Sunday morning to watch."

Instead he says that each one of you has received a special gift and that you are to use that special gift in serving one another. Three times in this passage Peter makes reference to "one another."

- Verse 8 speaks of *your love for one another*.
- Verse 9 told us to *be hospitable to one another*.
- Now in verse 10 we are told to employ our gifts *in serving one another*.

That tells me something about spiritual gifts. Spiritual gifts aren't about me doing something for my own edification or spirituality. They aren't even about doing something for the Lord. They are about me doing something for you and they are about you doing something for me. They are about serving one another.

That is important for you to know because there is some wrong thinking among Christians today about spiritual gifts. It is easy to spot the wrong thinking. Merely look for the emphasis. If the emphasis is upon my own growth or my own experience or my own effort or my own feelings, then it is a wrong emphasis.

We live in the "me" generation.

Comedian George Carlin does an amusing skit in which he points out the way magazine titles have changed in our lifetime. When we were young, there was a magazine called *Life*. Later on there came a new magazine called *People*. That is a smaller subsection than "Life." In more recent years there has come a magazine called "Us." I suppose that is as opposed to "them" and certainly doesn't include all of "people." Someone told me that now there is even a magazine called *Self*.

This self-centeredness has infected Christianity in America and it has impacted the way in which we view spiritual gifts.

This emphasis is seen today in the way people deal with the issue of tongues. I'm not going to get into the identification of tongues or all of the issues surrounding the modern charismatic movement, but if you look at what the Bible has to say about tongue in the book of Acts and in 1 Corinthians, you will see that the emphasis is upon how this gift was used or in how it is to be used or in how it is not to be used with respect to the service of others in the church.

1.   Spiritual Gifts are for One Another: *As each one has received a special gift, employ it in serving one another* (4:10).

The same thing is taught here in Peter's epistle. He teaches us that spiritual gifts are for one another. Your spiritual gift has been given for my benefit and my spiritual gift has been given for

127

your benefit. If I ever start to try to focus upon me benefitting from the use of my own spiritual gift, I have moved into an area of gross imbalance.

I know all about imbalance. I was sitting in an elder's meeting last week and all of a sudden the room started to spin around. It wasn't the room that was spinning. It was me. I had somehow contracted an inner ear infection and it wrecked havoc with my sense of balance. It felt like I was on one of those spinning, turning, dropping roller coasters and it got worse and worse and it just would not stop. It felt as though the whole world was moving, but in reality, the problem was in me.

Spiritual gifts are a wonderful thing and can greatly benefit the body. But when there is an imbalance that focuses upon the "me" then instead of edification there comes a great sickness and a troubling state of affairs. People start playing spiritual games:

"My gift is better than your gift."
"If you don't have my gift, then you are not even a part of the body." Paul actually addresses this problem in 1 Corinthians 12 when he talks about those who think that a certain member of the body is the only part that really counts. To combat such an idea he

asks, "What would it be like if the entire body were an eye or an ear?"

This brings us to our next point.

2.   Spiritual Gifts are Different: *Whoever speaks, let him speak, as it were, the utterances of God; whoever serves, let him do so as by the strength which God supplies* (4:11).

Peter could have mentioned any number of gifts. Paul gives several lists of the various gifts and each list is different. There is no exhaustive list of the gifts given in the Scriptures. People have tried to collate all of the different lists and put together a "master list" of all of the gifts, but the Bible never tells us that we have to do such a thing.

There is nothing wrong with this sort of study except that you might come away thinking that your particular list is all there is. I don't believe that to be the case. This list is not exhaustive; it is representative. Both Paul and Peter only mention a few of the gifts as a representative sampling.

The point that Peter is making here is that the gifts are different. There are some who speak and there are some who serve. Those are two general categories of gifts.

There are a lot of different ways to use

gifts in speaking and there are a lot of different ways to use gifts in serving. Both are good and both have a wide variety of ways in which they can be worked out.

3.   The way in which the gift works -- the mechanics of the gift -- is not nearly so important as is the source of the gift -- the One from whom the gift comes: *Whoever speaks, let him speak, as it were, the utterances of God; whoever serves, let him do so as by the strength which God supplies* (4:11).

When you speak, speak God's words. Make sure that what you are saying is what God is saying. I'm not just talking about Bible teaching, although this principle very obviously does apply to Bible teaching. One who teaches the Bible has a great obligation to teach God's word instead of lacing such teaching with his own opinion. This principle applies to all sorts of things that we speak.

- Words of encouragement.
- Words of exhortation.
- Words of praise.

Make sure that you are saying God's words. Let Him be the source of your speech and the Guider of your tongue.

Peter also has this same principle for those who serve. They are to serve, not from their own strength, but they are to serve in faith. They are to serve in the strength that God provides.

The result is that God is glorified. Peter points this out when he says that gifts are *so that in all things God may be glorified through Jesus Christ, to whom belongs the glory and dominion forever and ever (4:11)*. Spiritual gifts are merely a means to an end. The end is that God might be glorified. This takes place as we are filled with His Spirit so that His fruit is manifested through us.

The proper use of your spiritual gift will result in the fruit of the Spirit. This is why the Scriptures tell us that the gifts will cease, but that love will continue. Spiritual gifts are secondary. Balaam prophesied and yet he was a false prophet. His donkey spoke in tongues. Gifts will cease -- some of them already have. Don't get so caught up in various gifts to the point that you miss the Giver.

4.   The Gracious Nature of the Gifts: *Each one has received a special gift (4:10).*

When we are speaking of Spiritual Gifts, we ought not to lose sight of the fact that we are talking about gifts. A gift is something that you are given. You don't earn it. You don't deserve it. You are given it.

In our discussion of gifts, I would be remiss if I did not point you to the gift, the real gift from God. If you miss that gift, then all of the others are for naught. God's gift was wrapped in human flesh, born as a baby and growing up to walk our dirty streets and to die on our dirty cross as an atonement for our dirtiness. His body was broken and His blood was shed for you.

He was the perfect sacrifice for sins. He came to die in your place, taking your sins upon Himself and suffering the penalty for you sins. He is the Savior who saves the undeserving.

> *For by grace you have been saved through faith; and that not of yourselves, it is the gift of God; not as a result of works, so that no one may boast. (Ephesians 2:8-9).*

There are only two possible ways to be saved. The first is through the effort of another. The second is through self effort. One works. One does not.

You can be saved either by trusting in the One who died on the cross or you can attempt to be saved by trusting in yourself. In whom are you trusting? Upon what have you been depending? Your church attendance? Your abstinence from certain sins. Your involvement in some ritual or religious action? Your good works?

All of these may be commendable, but they do not save. To be saved, you need a Savior. Jesus is the only Savior. He is the ultimate fire fighter. Call upon Him today and He will save you.

Postscript:
My Retirement Day

*I have fought the good fight, I
have finished the course, I have
kept the faith (2 Timothy 4:7).*

In January, 2007, I ended a 29 year career,
starting with the Port Everglades Fire Fighters
which was then taken over by the Broward
County Fire Fighters and now is a part of the
larger family of the Broward Sheriff's Office
Department of Fire Rescue. It has been an honor
and a privilege to work with the best of the best.

There are some from that group with
whom I've been through major scenes, both in the
heat of fire as well as in various other responses
as we were called to save lives and property.
There are some of us who have burned together
and who have bled together. There have been

times when we risked our health, our well-being, and even our lives for one another. There is a bond forged in such experiences that goes far beyond the norm in human relations.

My own reflections on this career have been colored by the fact that there was once One who sacrificed His own life for me, dying in my place. Such a sacrifice cannot be forgotten. His name is Jesus Christ -- in a very real way, I consider Him to be the ultimate in Fire Rescue. He both is my Lord and my Savior. My Rescuer.

We regularly conduct emergency preplans of how we are going to react to catastrophic situations. This life is only temporary and we are only practicing and preparing for eternity. It is only the fool who does not prepare for the inevitable, so I hope that each of my brothers and sisters will use the same sort of due care in their own personal lives that they typically take on the job.

Even though I am a pastor and a Bible teacher, I don't like to come across as "preachy" and Christianity is not about trying to show oneself as being better than everyone else. To the contrary, a Christian is, by definition, one who has come to the realization that he will never be able to measure up to that which he ought to be. Hence the need for a Savior; One who gave Himself on my behalf, that I might find real acceptance.

I take a great delight in introducing friends to friends. When you find a rich, personal friendship, it is only natural to want to share that

136

with others. If this book has caught your interest and you would like to discuss it further, drop me a line. I would love to take the opportunity to introduce you to the best friend of all.

CPSIA information can be obtained
at www.ICGtesting.com
Printed in the USA
LVOW13s0903301017

554275LV00004B/402/P